MR KEY'S SHORTER POTTED BRIEF, BRIEF LIVES

MR KEY'S
Shorter Potted
Brief, Brief Lives

FRANK KEY

Constable • London

CONSTABLE

First published in Great Britain in 2015 by Constable

A CIP catalogue record for this book
is available from the British Library.

ISBN 978-1-47211-523-2 (hardback)
ISBN: 978-1-47211-524-9 (ebook)

Typeset in Baskerville by Photoprint, Torquay
Printed and bound in Great Britain by CPI Group (UK) Ltd,
Croydon CR0 4YY

Papers used by Constable are from well-managed forests and
other sustainable sources

MIX
Paper from
responsible sources
FSC® C104740

Constable
is an imprint of
Little, Brown Book Group
Carmelite House
50 Victoria Embankment
London EC4Y 0DZ

An Hachette UK Company
www.hachette.co.uk

www.littlebrown.co.uk

For Stephanie Thomson

Abercrombie, Lascelles (English essayist) Abercrombie suggested that it was the popularity of Wordsworth ... in a duel by Ezra Pound ... beyond a certain point ... the choice of weapons ... the poets throw, should ... each other.

Branovich, Roman (The ...) ... Branovich employs a First ... of thirty thousand euros ... that, for certainty, that the ... earth are always filled with ...

Adam (the first man) ... the seventeenth century, ... the body of Adam was ... ... potent than crystal and as ... vessels and utensils ... ... coursed through the pores ... liquors of various colours ... ... potency. Some of these liquors ... ... Every motion of Adam's ... harmonies. Every creature ...

Abercrombie, Lascelles (English poet, 1881–1938). Abercrombie suggested poets should aspire to the simplicity of Wordsworth, and as a result was challenged to a duel by Ezra Pound, who told him 'stupidity carried beyond a certain point becomes a public menace'. Given the choice of weapons, Abercrombie proposed that the poets throw unsold copies of their own books at each other.

Abramovich, Roman (Russian oligarch, b. 1966). Abramovich employs a Fruit Manager on an annual salary of thirty thousand euros. The Fruit Manager is responsible for ensuring that the fruit bowls on Abramovich's yacht are always filled with washed and ready-to-eat fruit.

Adam (Edenite first man, 4004–3074 BC). According to the seventeenth-century mystic Antoinette Bourignon, the body of Adam was more pure, translucent, and transparent than crystal, and as light and buoyant as air. In it were vessels and streams of light, which entered and exuded through the pores. The vessels were charged with liquors of various colours of intense brilliancy and transparency. Some of these fluids were water, milk, wine, and fire. Every motion of Adam's body produced ineffable harmonies. Every creature obeyed him, nothing could resist or injure him. He was taller than men of this time. His hair was short, curled, and approaching black. He had a little down on his lower lip. In his stomach was a clear fluid, like water in a crystal bowl, in which tiny eggs developed themselves, like bubbles in wine, as he glowed with the ardour of Divine charity. When he strongly desired that others should unite with him in the work of praise, he deposited some of those eggs, which hatched, and from one of them emerged his consort, Eve. *See* Eve

Adams, John (American politician and POTUS, 1735–1826). The second President of the United States had a pet dog named Satan. His son, John Quincy Adams, the sixth President, kept silkworms.

Adams, Richard (English writer, b. 1920). When the *Watership Down* author's later novel *The Girl In A Swing* appeared in 1980, it met with an unfavourable review from A. N. Wilson. Five years later, Adams and Wilson bumped into each other at a party. The author insisted that the critic justify his review. Wilson confessed that he could not recall what he had written, whereupon Adams recited the entire thousand-word piece from memory. When Wilson still failed to explain himself, he was bombarded with letters, telephone calls, and a cassette recording, until he begged Adams to desist.

Aladdin (Arabian folk tale hero). According to Thomas De Quincey, in the tale of Aladdin 'after the possession of the lamp has been once secured by a pure accident, the story ceases to move. All the rest is a mere record of upholstery; how this saloon was finished today, and that window on the next day, with no fresh incident whatever.'

Albert (German, Prince Consort of England, 1819–61). Prince Albert was deeply involved with the Great Exhibition of 1851 and counted it as a personal triumph. On 5 July, he persuaded Queen Victoria to join him in a visit where they mingled with the crowds. Exhibitors were obviously keen to bring their wares to the attention of the royal couple, and at one point Victoria and Albert were confronted by a gathering of dentists, brandishing sets of false teeth in their hands and waving them at the startled couple.

Alexandros I (Greek king, 1893–1920). Alexandros died aged twenty-seven after being bitten by one of his pet monkeys. *See* Barrymore, John

Alice, Princess of Battenberg (English princess, 1885–1969). The mother of Prince Philip, Duke of Edinburgh, was a religious maniac who liked to dress as a nun. Indeed, she attended the coronation of her daughter-in-law dressed in a wimple and plain grey robes, and founded an order of nursing nuns. Early in life she had delusions of a sexual relationship with Christ, which her doctor described as a 'neurotic-pre-psychotic libidinous condition', though Queen Mary put it more simply by saying 'religion had gone to her head'. She chain-smoked and enjoyed playing canasta.

Allegro, John (English archaeologist and scholar, 1923–88). Allegro was a respected scholar of the Dead Sea Scrolls who, during the 1960s, concocted the theory that Christianity had originated as an ancient sex-cult fuelled by hallucinogenic mushrooms. Many of the major figures in the Bible were in fact to be understood as

3

'walking mushrooms'. He propounded his ideas in a series of best-selling books which fit with the temper of the times, including *The Sacred Mushroom And The Cross* (1970). Turning his attention to the Old Testament, Allegro explained that Jehovah was 'a mighty penis in the heavens' which 'ejaculated semen upon the furrows of Mother Earth'.

American Woman, An (American writer, nineteenth century). 'An American Woman' was the anonymous *nom de plume* chosen by the author of *The Ladies' Vase or, Polite Manual For Young Ladies*, an 1849 tome in which she counselled: 'If you wish to become weak-headed, nervous, and good for nothing, read novels. I have seen an account of a young lady, who had become so nervous and excitable, in consequence of reading novels, that her head would be turned by the least appearance of danger, real or imaginary. As she was riding in a carriage over a bridge, in company with her mother and sister, she became frightened at some fancied danger, caught hold of the reins, and backed the carriage off the bridge, down a precipice, dashing them to pieces.'

Amundsen, Roald (Norwegian explorer, 1872–1928). From an early age, Amundsen was wholly obsessed by the idea of polar exploration. He said that what he found most compelling in the accounts he read was the suffering undergone by the explorers. Mindful of this, he slept with his bedroom window open throughout the year, and engaged in exhausting winter skiing trips. By the time he signed up for the army, his physique was so impressive that the doctor made him parade naked as an example to the other recruits.

Anderson, John Henry (Scottish magician, 1814–74). The first magician to pull a rabbit out of a hat, Anderson also did a trick which he described as 'a Grand Ambidexterological Illusion with 12 Handkerchiefs, into which will be introduced the Enchanted Loaf and Learned Bottle, the Animated Orange and the Invisible Pigeon'.

Anning, Mary (English palaeontologist, 1799–1847). Mary Anning was born in humble circumstances and lived most of her life in poverty, yet made a name for herself as a palaeontologist. At the age of eleven she discovered the first complete ichthyosuar skeleton, and later the first pterodactyl fossil. She was reportedly a 'dull-witted baby', but at a horse fair in Lyme Regis, sheltering from a storm under an elm tree, she and three adults were struck by lightning. The adults were killed, but the infant Mary Anning thereafter 'became lively and intelligent'.

Archer, Fred (English champion jockey, 1857–86). A friend recalled: 'Somehow, Archer seemed to fascinate people. I know he did me. Perhaps it was the glamour of his wonderful riding; yet, I think it was his personality . . . His end came all too soon in 1886. I was at the Eagle-Farm race-course, Brisbane, Queensland, when the news came. It cast a gloom over the gathering. One heard whispers of "Archer's dead. Archer's shot himself. Poor Fred." The last race he rode was on Tommy Tittlemouse at Lewes. He had been ill all the week, and was advised to go home. He was terribly ill when he reached Newmarket. He had a pistol in his room by his bedside, and in a fit of delirium shot himself before he could be prevented. Wasting and Turkish baths did it.'

Armstrong, Louis (American jazz musician, 1901–71). Aged twelve, Armstrong saw in the New Year 1913 by firing a stolen revolver in the air. Apprehended by the police, he was sent to the New Orleans Colored Waifs' Home For Boys, whose principal later thought to divert the young tearaway by presenting him with a trumpet.

Arthur, T. S. (American writer and temperance advocate, 1809–85). Arthur was a tireless advocate against the demon drink, and made the unlikely claim that he had once held in his hands the brain of a sozzled alcoholic who had been decapitated under the wheels of a speeding train just three minutes earlier. The impact had, it seemed, 'evolved' the brain from the skull, and Arthur happened to be at hand to pick it up and examine it. Edgar Allan Poe, who knew Arthur, said he was 'uneducated and too fond of mere vulgarities to please a refined taste'.

Arthy, Nathaniel (English undergraduate, nineteenth century). The sole biographical information we have on Arthy is that he entered Caius College, Cambridge as an undergraduate in 1854 and thereafter 'made a failure of his life'. *See* Malthus, Thomas

Atherton, Gertrude (American writer, 1857–1948). Atherton declined an invitation to meet Oscar Wilde (q.v.), having been shown his photograph. 'His mouth covered half his face, the most lascivious, coarse, repulsive mouth I had ever seen. I might stand it in a large crowded

6

drawing-room, but not in a parlour, eight by eight, lit by three tallow candles. I should feel as if I were under the sea, pursued by some bloated monster of the deep.'

Atholl Oakeley, Sir Edward (English wrestler, writer, and organiser of 'rugged holiday cruises', 1900–87). To build up his physique, Atholl Oakeley followed a regime devised by the giant Estonian wrestler Georg Hackenschmidt, which involved drinking eleven pints of milk every day. Many years later, Hackenschmidt told him that the quantity of milk prescribed was 'a misprint'. *See* Hawker, Stephen

Attlee, Clement (English politician and Prime Minister, 1883–1967). Attlee took a dim view of his illustrious predecessor William Gladstone (q.v.). 'He really was a frightful old prig,' he wrote. 'Fancy writing a letter proposing marriage including a sentence of 140 words all about the Almighty. He was a dreadful person.' The sentence from Gladstone's letter to his future wife reads: 'I seek much in a wife in gifts better than those of our human pride, and am also sensible that she can find little in me, sensible that, were you to treat this note as the offspring of utter presumption, I must not be surprised: sensible that the life I invite you to share, even if it be not attended, as I trust it is not, with peculiar disadvantages of an outward kind, is one, I do not say unequal to your deserts, for that were saying little, but liable at best to changes and perplexities and pains which, for myself, I contemplate without apprehension, but to which it is perhaps selfishness in the main, with the sense of inward dependence counteracting an opposite sense of my too real unworthiness, which would make me contribute to expose another – and that other!'

Aubrey, John (English writer and antiquary, 1626–97). It is a wonder Aubrey lived long enough to write his *Brief Lives*. He had an ague shortly after he was born, and a grievous ague, aged three or four. He vomited for twelve hours every fortnight for years. At eight he 'had an issue in the coronal sutor of my head which continued running until I was twenty-one'. One October he had a violent fever and at fifteen or sixteen the measles, followed by a dangerous fall from his uncle's horse, then smallpox. At twenty he fell and broke a rib and was afraid it might cause an apostumation. Then he was shipwrecked, had a terrible fit of the spleen, piles, and near-fatal laesio in testiculo. Soon after an impostume broke his head, he was attacked with a sword, and twice nearly drowned. Also a drunkard tried to kill him in the street.

Babbage, Charles (English polymath, 1791–1871). When he was not busy inventing the computer, Babbage was much exercised by what he called 'street nuisances'. He listed 'Instruments of torture permitted by the Government to be in daily and nightly use in the streets of London: Organs, Brass bands, Fiddlers, Harps, Harpsichords, Hurdy-gurdies, Flageolots, Drums, Bagpipes, Accordians, Halfpenny whistles, Tom toms, Trumpets, Shouting out objects for sale, Religious canting, and Psalm-singing.' He added a list of 'Encouragers of street music: Tavern-keepers, Public-houses, Gin-shops, Beer-shops, Coffee-shops, Servants, Children, Visitors from the country, Ladies of doubtful virtue, and Occasionally titled ladies; but these are almost invariably of recent elevation, and deficient in that taste which their sex usually possess.'

Bach, Johann Sebastian (German composer, 1685–1750). Conducting a rehearsal one day, Bach was so outraged when a member of the orchestra played a wrong note that he plucked off his wig and threw it at the malefactor.

Baden-Powell, Robert (English scoutmaster, 1857–1941). Baden-Powell's favoured method of crossing the road was to stride forth, looking to neither left nor right, sure in the conviction that the 'foot slogger' had as much right to the King's highway as any motorist. If, as a result, he 'gets it in the back', he dies asserting his right. That is not 'blank foolishness'. 'That's British.'

Bains, Hardial (Indian Marxist-Leninist revolutionary, 1939–97). In the 1970s, having decided that Maoism was an imperialist reactionary deviation and that Albania was the only true socialist state, Bains turned his hand to writing song lyrics. 'We Sing For The Future', for example, begins:

> In utter chaos the old order spews out unlimited
> decadence and parasitism.
> It brings disaster to mankind and fights against
> progress with unprecedented ferocity.
> Stricken by all kinds of sickness, this system's in all-
> sided crisis with economics at the base.
> Spiritual and cultural devastation – the crisis is social
> and political too.

These and other words were set to jaunty tunes by Cornelius Cardew (q.v.). Cardew himself provided the lyrics for his 1971 piece '10,000 Nails In The Coffin Of Imperialism', for voice, hammer and nails, and blocks of wood.

Baird, John Logie (Scottish inventor, 1888–1946). Before inventing the television, Baird tried his hand at his own varieties of jam, honey, and soap, and a patent sock. The first television was a makeshift Heath Robinson affair, mounted on a washstand. The base of the motor was a tea-chest, the projection lamp was housed in a biscuit-tin,

10

scanning discs were cut from cardboard, and the rest of the apparatus consisted of fourpenny cycle lenses, scrapwood, darning needles, sealing wax and string.

Bakunin, Mikhail (Russian anarchist, 1814–76). Bakunin was one of history's great smokers. During his final months in Locarno, suffering from kidney, bladder, and prostate problems and barely able to sleep, he was joined by a young anarchist admirer. She recalled, 'His only luxuries were tobacco and tea. He smoked all day without stop, and all night as well, except for short periods of sleep, when the pain let him sleep. He smoked while drinking tea. He bought tobacco pounds at a time, or so it seemed, and stacked it in piles on all the tables. "If you are here when I die," he often said when lighting a cigarette, "take care now and do not forget to stick a cigarette in my mouth, so that I can take a last puff before I die."' Bakunin did occasionally bestir himself to encourage the many children in the house to light bonfires and dance around them 'like savages', though having set the blazes going he would abandon both fires and children and wander back to the 'narrow iron bed' in his room.

Balcolm, Julia (Fictional character, d. 1857). Julia Balcolm was one of the most memorable characters of nineteenth-century fiction. She appeared in *Withered Leaves From Memory's Garland* (1857) by Abigail Stanley Hanna: 'Next to Rosa Whittier sat Julia Balcolm, with saddened expression of countenance and large deep blue eyes that gazed upon you with a deeper expression of melancholy in their glances than is usual to the merry age of childhood, and elicited your sympathy ere you knew her history. Julia was a cripple. She was drawn to school

11

by an older sister with rosy cheeks, bright flashing black eyes, and a sprightly animated countenance, and carried into the school-room in the arms of her teacher, or some of the older scholars. And so she came, year after year, mingling with the merry group. But where is she now? Yon little mound of heaped up earth covers her remains, and a narrow marble slab tells the place of her repose, and we can but hope she who was denied the privilege of walking on earth may now soar on angel's wings. This dear child was obliged to crawl from place to place after her more favoured companions, dragging her useless perished limbs behind her. But He who careth for us knew what was best for her, and we cannot doubt His infinite wisdom.'

Ballard, J. G. (English writer, 1930–2009). Ballard said: 'The great thing about science fiction is that nobody lives in Hampstead.'

Bangs, John Kendrick (American writer, 1862–1922). In *The Booming Of Acre Hill*, Bangs invented an essential piece of kit for the night-owl writer. 'The Jarley Ready Writing-Desk for Night Use, for instance, was a really remarkable conception. Its chief value lay in the saving of gas and midnight oil to impecunious writers which its use was said to bring about, and when fully equipped consisted simply of a writing-table with all the appliances and conveniences thereof treated with phosphorus in such a manner that in the blackest of darkness they could all be seen readily. The ink even was phosphorescent. The paper was luminous in the dark. The penholders, pens, pen-wipers, mucilage-bottle, everything, in fact, that an author really needs for the production of literature, save ideas, were so prepared that they could not fail to be visible to the weakest eye in the darkest night.' *See* Blegvad, Peter

Barbellion, W. N. P. (English diarist, real name Bruce Frederick Cummings, 1889–1919). One of the tragedies of Barbellion's short life was that he abandoned the idea of writing a work to be entitled *How Cats Spend Their Time.* *See* De Clifford, Nerea

Baring-Gould, Sabine (English clergyman and writer, 1834–1924). Baring-Gould was the prolific author of over a thousand works, including a sixteen-volume *Lives Of The Saints*, ghost stories, the hymn 'Onward, Christian Soldiers', and studies of werewolves, grave desecration, and cannibalism, all written while standing up at his desk. As a young curate he was dispatched to Dalton in Swaledale, a place beset by so remarkable an amount of mud that locals called it Dalton i' t' Muck. Baring-Gould was struck by the stupidity of his congregation, and reflected that 'the natives were perhaps affected by the mud'. It proved useful preparation for the time, some years later, when, lost while hiking across Dartmoor in the night, he sank up to his armpits in a bog.

Barnes, Albert (American chemist and art collector, 1872–1951). Barnes amassed a huge modern art collection, but his hatred of the art world establishment meant that he refused or limited access to scholars who travelled to Pennsylvania to see it. One art historian was made to wait outside while his dog was admitted. T. S. Eliot's request earned the one-word reply 'Nuts!'.

Barrymore, John (American actor, 1882–1942). Barrymore kept a menagerie of pets including an opossum, a kinkajou, deer, cats, dogs, and hundreds of exotic birds. One of his favourites was a vulture named Maloney, who would perch on his shoulder and preen his moustache and eyebrows. He also had a monkey called Clementine, which bit everybody except Barrymore himself. Clementine would sit quite still, gazing adoringly at the actor for hours. A vet eventually explained that the monkey was transfixed by the fumes of alcohol reeking from her master. After Barrymore was persuaded to give Clementine away to a zoo, he used to visit her there and breathe on her. *See* Caruso, Enrico

Bastiat, Frédéric (French political theorist, 1801–50). Bastiat was the author of the satirical pamphlet 'A Petition From The Manufacturers Of Candles, Tapers, Lanterns, Sticks, Street Lamps, Snuffers, And Extinguishers, And From Producers Of Tallow, Oil, Resin, Alcohol, And Generally Of Everything Connected With Lighting', in which he pleaded with the Assembly (of which he was a member) 'to be so good as to pass a law requiring the closing of all windows, dormers, skylights, inside and outside shutters, curtains, casements, bull's-eyes, deadlights, and blinds – in short, all openings, holes, chinks, and fissures through which the light of the sun is wont to enter houses.'

Bateman, Mary (English poisoner, 1768–1809). Mary Bateman was responsible for the Prophetic Hen of Leeds hoax in 1806. A hen began to lay eggs on which 'Christ Is Coming' was written. The alleged witch had used acid to write on the eggs and then reinserted them into the

14

hen. Three years later she was hanged for poisoning Rebecca Porigo, who had asked for her help in lifting a curse.

Baxter, Jeff 'Skunk' (American musician, b. 1948). Following his stints as guitarist with Steely Dan and The Doobie Brothers, Baxter became a senior ballistic weapons adviser to the George W. Bush administration.

Bayliss, Peter (English actor, 1922–2002). Bayliss' dying words were 'My spacesuit has developed a fault.' He often went out accompanied by an invisible pet dog. For many years the message on his answering machine was his impersonation of a parrot saying 'Peter Bayliss is not available. He's gone out to get my bird seed.'

Bechstein, Johann Matthäus (German naturalist, 1757–1822). Bechstein attempted to write down the song of the nightingale. *The Athenaeum No. 1467* commented 'one would think the music hardly worth having, if it really sounded as it looks upon paper, transcribed thus by Bechstein, from whom it is quoted by Broderip':

> Zozozozozozozozozozozozozo zirrharding
> Hezezezezezezezezezezezezezeze cowar ho dze hoi
> Higaigaigaigaigaigaigaigaigaigai, guaiagai coricor dzio
> dzio pi

Beckett, Samuel (Irish writer, 1906–89). Beckett's favourite childhood pastime was to climb to the top of a tall tree and then fling himself to the ground.

Beddoes, Thomas Lovell (English poet, 1803–49). As a young man, Beddoes fell in love with German philosophy and travelled to Bavaria. He was expelled for making intemperate speeches, and the deportation order described him thus: 'Height 5' 7", hair light brown, eyebrows fair, eyes very dark, nose long and quite pointed, mouth large, chin prominent, face oval, complexion pale, build slight, carelessly dressed either in the English manner or as a swashbuckling German hero, one boot black, the other red, and on one of them a gold or gilt spur. Speaks bad German, has fair moustache and bad teeth.' When Beddoes returned to England he visited his relatives riding a donkey and then tried to set fire to Drury Lane Theatre with a burning five-pound note.

Beeton, Isabella (English writer and domestic goddess, 1836–65). Mrs Beeton did not just know about household management. She was surprisingly well informed about pigs. 'From the grossness of his feeding, from the large amount of aliment he consumes, his gluttonous way of eating it, from his slothful habits, laziness, and indulgence in sleep, the pig is particularly liable to disease, and especially indigestion, heartburn and affections of the skin,' she wrote. 'To counteract the consequence of a violation of the physical laws, a powerful monitor in the brain of a pig teaches him to seek for relief and medicine.'

Bell, Alexander Graham (Scottish inventor, 1847–1922). Having invented the telephone, Bell's next step was to devise telephone etiquette. He suggested that the appropriate greeting when answering a call was to shout 'Ahoy!'.

Bellas, Jane (English market-stall worker, b. 1979). Jane Bellas was charged by Cumbria police with possession of a knife. Her defence that she needed the knife for her work on a stall at a food market looked likely to fail when the local council found no trace that she had a stall-holder's licence. She was acquitted, however, when an eyewitness came forward to say she had been seen 'tinkering with a generator, while handling a sausage'.

Benn, Tony (English politician, 1925–2014). In 1883, Benn's great-great-uncle, who was the father of the actress Margaret Rutherford, murdered his own father by bashing him on the head with a chamberpot.

Bennett, Arnold (English writer, 1867–1931). Bennett believed that 'pavement' was one of the most beautiful words in the English language.

Bentham, Jeremy (English philosopher, 1748–1832). Bentham's corpse is famously preserved and kept in a display case at University College London. When experiments were being conducted on the body immediately after Bentham's death, James Mill observed that the head exuded a type of oil which seemed almost unfreezable. He conceived the idea of using it to lubricate the workings of chronometers used by those travelling at high latitudes. To date this has not been put into practice.

Berkeley, Bishop (Irish philosopher, 1685–1753). Like many men of his time, Berkeley was immune to the sublime grandeur of mountains. Finding himself on the Mont Cenis Pass in the Alps, he was 'put out of humour by the most horrible precipices' and declared that 'every object that here presents itself is excessively miserable'.

Bernard of Clairvaux (French abbot and saint, 1090–1153). Saint Bernard, the founder of the Cistercian order, warned the faithful specifically about jugglers: 'A man fond of jugglers will soon enough possess a wife whose name is Poverty. If it happens that the tricks of jugglers are forced upon your notice, endeavour to avoid them, and think of other things.'

Bernhardt, Sarah (French actress, 1844–1923). Sarah Bernhardt kept a menagerie of exotic pets, including a boa constrictor which she shot dead after it swallowed one of her cushions. *See* Charles I

Bertolotto, Louis (Italian flea circus proprietor, 1802–87). On Regent Street in London in 1833, Bertolotto exhibited 'The Extraordinary Exhibition Of The Industrious Fleas'. The programme included a vivid re-enactment of the Siege of Antwerp: 'Representing the Fort, besieged and defended by Fleas, with Fire Arms, such as Cannons, Obus, Mortars, &c., which they set fire to, and make sufficient report to be audible all over the room, although the Gold Cannons &c. are not larger than a common Pin. General Chàsse and Mareschal Gerard riding on Fleas, and encouraging their respective Soldier, i.e. the flea, to victory'.

Betty, William (English actor, 1791–1874). Betty, known as 'the Young Roscius', was a child actor who was enormously popular in the early nineteenth century. It was said he could play convincingly any part, including elderly men and women. So great was his celebrity that Lord Byron dubbed the phenomenon 'Rosciomania'. When he appeared on stage in Birmingham, it was reported that not only the inhabitants of that city but the 'iron and coal workers' of the entire Midlands were agog to see him. 'One man, more curious or more idle than his fellows, determined to leave his work, and see the prodigy with his own eyes. Having so resolved, he proceeded, although in the middle of the week, to put on a clean shirt and a clean face, and would even have anticipated the Saturday's shaving. The unwonted hue of the shirt and face were portents not to be disregarded.' Betty retired from the stage very early, rarely acted thereafter, and became 'a person of no particular note in the world'.

Beverland, Hadrian (Dutch philosopher and classical scholar, 1650–1716). When Beverland published *Original Sin*, his survey of the sexual abnormalities of the ancient world, in 1679, it was denounced by the authorities at Leyden University as 'abominable and scandalous' and 'an abortion from depraved brains'. He was banished from Holland, never to return. He spent the rest of his life in London where, shortly before he died, he wrote 'The Song of the Borts of Pray':

I have no Wife
The Devil Upon Two Crutches
Chear! Chear! Hier
Carry me to Hell.
I do not know my L. where Hell is: But if it may
    please your L. I carry you to the Devil.
Go unto the Devil Tavern.
What upon Crutches!
I am very Old, if it may please your L.
No Old Devil can please me. Have you no younger
    Devils in Hell?

19

Yes, Long Brown, who carries little Davits upon his
    Shoulders:
What is become of little Gibson?

Bierce, Ambrose (American writer, 1842–vanished 1913).
Bierce was one of thirteen children all of whose given
names began with the letter A. His parents, Marcus
Aurelius Bierce and Laura Sherwood Bierce, of Horse Cave
Creek, Meigs County, Ohio, named their children, from
the oldest to the youngest: Abigail, Amelia, Ann Maria,
Addison, Aurelius, Augustus, Almeda, Andrew, Albert,
Ambrose, Arthur, and the twins Adelia and Aurelia. *See*
Tollemache-Tollemache, Ralph William Lyonel

Birch, Thomas (English historian, 1705–66). Birch was a
keen angler. In order to deceive the fish he wished to
catch, he devised a costume which made him look like an
old tree. He assumed that the telltale movements of his
arms casting the rod would be mistaken by the fish for
branches stirring in the wind. It is not known if Birch's
disguise resembled, in particular, a birch tree.

Bisset, Samuel (Scottish animal trainer, eighteenth century). Bisset read an article about a 'learned horse' in
Germany and resolved to try his hand at training animals.
He had immediate success with horses and dogs, and proceeded to teach monkeys to walk on tightropes and play
the barrel organ. Continuing with the musical theme, he
devised a 'Cat's Opera', with a group of cats playing the
dulcimer and squealing. He taught canaries, linnets, and
sparrows to spell, turkeys to dance, and turtles to fetch
and carry things. He also exhibited an educated goldfish.
His most successful pupil, however, was the Learned Pig,

also known as the Scientific Pig, which began a fad for such pigs throughout Europe.

Blair, Tony (British politician and Prime Minister, b. 1953). In 2001 Blair and his wife Cherie underwent a Mayan rebirthing ceremony at a pyramid on a Mexican beach. Wearing bathing costumes, they took a steam bath while praying to the Four Winds. Then, while Mayan chants were chanted, they smeared mud and the juice of papayas and melons over each other, before screaming aloud to express the pain of rebirth. Although on holiday, Blair was still in charge of the country at the time. He had left office by the time he appeared, in white robes, on the banks of the River Jordan for the baptism of Rupert Murdoch's youngest children in 2010.

Blake, William (English artist and writer, 1757–1827). A visitor to their home one day was disconcerted to find William Blake and his wife Catherine sitting together in the garden stark naked. 'We are Adam and Eve,' the visionary declared. Blake had many other visitors, in the form of the spirits of various historical and Biblical personages, whose portraits he painted. Kings Edward III and Richard III, Mark Antony, and Lot were among his spectral guests, though to Blake's dismay he was never visited by Satan.

Blears, Hazel (English politician, b. 1956). Diminutive Hazel Blears, Labour Minister Without Portfolio during the Blair administration and keen motorcyclist, appeared as a child actress in the classic kitchen sink film drama *A Taste Of Honey* (1961). Her part, uncredited, was that of 'street urchin'.

Blegvad, Peter (American musician and illustrator, b. 1951). Blegvad is the inventor of 'angel trap stationery', paper painted with symbols and impregnated with scents designed to attract various powers and dominions of the air to aid the act of composition.

Blot, Pierre (French chef, 1818–74). In the 1860s Blot was briefly lionised by New York society as a celebrity chef bringing French cooking to the United States. He wrote extensively on the preparation of potatoes. The tide turned when *The Galaxy*, for which he had written a column, said that his published recipe book was filled with 'unintelligible and useless' instructions. By the time he died he was neglected and forgotten.

Bloy, Léon (French writer, 1846–1917). As a child, Bloy was told by his mother: 'My dear child, it is true you're an ox, but an ox whose bellowings will one day astonish Christendom!'

Blunkett, David (English politician, b. 1947). In 2004 Blunkett felt the need to insist 'I do not want people going out inciting others against devil worshippers.' Later, in an eerie echo of the August 1892 cow attack on William Gladstone (q.v.), Blunkett was attacked by a cow in Derbyshire on his birthday in 2009. He suffered a broken rib and bruising. On this occasion the cow was not shot. *See* Bristow, Alan

Bohman, Adam and Jonathan (English musicians b. 1959 and 1961) The Bohman Brothers are an electro-acoustic improvisation duo whose stage equipment resembles the aftermath of an explosion in an ironmongery. While eliciting amplified sounds from such objects as cheese-graters, toilet plungers, plastic funnels, and shoe brushes, one or both of them will recite the text from a mundane source such as a pizza delivery leaflet. The result is both comic and terrifying. It has been said of the Bohman Brothers that 'they can show you fear in the sponge from the drainer'.

Boorde, Andrew (English physician and writer, *c.* 1490– 1549). In his manual *Dyetary of Helth* published in 1542, Boorde warned against the taking of daytime naps. If, however, a man felt compelled to take a snooze after a meal, 'then let him stand, and lean and sleep against a cupboard'. *See* Delacroix, Eugène

Borges, Jorge Luis (Argentinian writer, 1899–1986). In 1946, Borges was appointed to the post of Chief Poultry Inspector for the Buenos Aires municipal market. He resigned immediately.

Boswell, James (Scottish writer, 1740–95). Boswell's preferred method of getting up in the morning was to leap out of bed and to cut two or three brisk capers around the room. He found this expelled the phlegm from his heart, gave his blood a free circulation and made his spirits flow, so he immediately felt happy. *See* Delacroix, Eugène

Bottle, J. M. W. (English memory man, 1875–1956). Bottle was known professionally as Datas, the Memory Man, an overnight success from his first variety theatre performance in 1901, and the acknowledged inspiration for similar figures in *The 39 Steps* by John Buchan and *The Man Who Knew Too Much* by Alfred Hitchcock. The real Datas was particularly intrigued by gruesome deaths, murders, executions, and disasters. It was said of him, 'He has little more education than the average labourer, is scarcely more articulate, writes in no better style, he is by no means well-read or in any degree cultured.'

Boyle, Robert (Irish natural philosopher, 1627–91). Among his other achievements, Boyle discovered luminous meat. In *Some Observations About Shining Flesh, Both of Veal and Pullet, and That without any Sensible Putrefaction in those Bodies* (1672), he wrote, 'Yesterday, when I was about to go to bed, an amanuensis of mine, accustomed to make observations, informed me, that one of the servants of the house, going upon some occasion to the larder, was frightened by something luminous, that she saw (not withstanding the darkness of the place) where the meat had been hung up before. Whereupon, suspending for a while my going to rest, I presently sent for the meat into my chamber, and caused it to be placed in a corner of the room capable of being made considerably dark, and then I plainly saw, both with wonder and delight, that the joint of meat did, in divers places, shine like rotten wood or stinking fish; which was so uncommon a sight, that I had presently thoughts of inviting you to be a sharer of the pleasures of it.'

Bradlaugh, Charles (English atheist, 1833–91). Bradlaugh held the view, unfashionable in the Victorian era, that the books of the Bible had their origins in the ravings of 'illiterate half-starved visionaries in some dark corner of a Graeco-Syrian slum'.

Bradshaw, Ben (English politician, b. 1960). When he was Under-Secretary of State for Environment, Food and Rural Affairs in 2005, Bradshaw was asked what plans the government had for cormorants. In his reply he claimed that cormorants fared much better under Labour administrations than they did under the Conservatives. Labour, he said, was good for all birds, not just cormorants.

Brahms, Johannes (German composer, 1833–97). For many years Brahms was execrated as a man who tortured and killed cats for pleasure. It was said that he would shoot them with a 'Bohemian sparrow-slaying bow' (given to him by Anton Dvořák), reel them in through the window, shove them into a bag and, while they struggled and gradually suffocated, transcribe their dying howls and groans into musical notation, passages he would then insert into his compositions. In fact this was a malicious fabrication spread by Richard Wagner, repeated by biographers (and cat lovers).

Branden, Nathaniel (Canadian writer and psychotherapist, b. 1930). According to Nathaniel Branden, Ayn Rand is the greatest human being who has ever lived, *Atlas Shrugged* is the greatest human achievement in the history of the world, and Ayn Rand designated Nathaniel

Branden as her intellectual heir so he is to be accorded only marginally less reverence than Ayn Rand herself.

Bristow, Alan (English helicopter entrepreneur, 1923–2009). As a test pilot, Bristow survived innumerable helicopter crashes, including six engine failures in one day. He regularly got into fights, and once threw Douglas Bader into a swimming pool, calling him a 'tin-legged git'. At the age of seventy-five, he started a new business producing his patented water bed for cows. *See* Chesterton, G. K.

Brooke, Charles (English, Rajah of Sarawak, 1829–1917). Brooke was the epitome of the spirit that built the British Empire. An austere character, he considered jam 'effeminate' and replaced his glass eye with one taken from a stuffed albatross.

Brooke, Rupert (English poet, 1887–1915). Brooke was killed by a gnat, which bit him on the lip when he was sailing to Gallipoli as part of the British Mediterranean Force. He died of blood poisoning before he got there.

Brooker, Gary (English musician, b. 1945). On tour as part of Eric Clapton's band (with support act Chas & Dave), the Procol Harum founder gained the nickname 'Hornby'. Temporarily eschewing the rock & roll lifestyle, Brooker was caught playing with an electric train set in his hotel room. He owns a large gorilla made of granite which he calls 'Stephen Fry'.

Brooks, Rebekah (English journalist, b. 1968). During the great phone hacking trial of 2013/14, it was alleged that Brooks' husband Charlie, anticipating a police search of the couple's London flat, concealed a bag filled with various potentially incriminating items behind the bins in the basement car park. It was found by a conscientious cleaner, who handed it in to the police. In addition to laptop computers, mobile phones, and pornographic DVDs, the bag contained a tube of toothpaste, a conker, and a copy of the newsletter of the British Kunekune Pig Society. He was acquitted of a charge of attempting to pervert the course of justice.

Brown, Joe (English musician, b. 1941). At the outset of his career, Brown was managed by Larry Parnes, who liked to rechristen his charges with names like Billy Fury, Marty Wilde, and Georgie Fame. The name chosen for – and rejected by – Brown was Almer Twitch.

Buchanan, Joseph Rodes (American physician and spiritualist, 1814–99). After much experience of table-rapping and séances, Buchanan became convinced that dead doctors were more effective than living ones. 'The late Dr. Wells of Brooklyn has been giving diagnoses and prescriptions through the telegraph,' he wrote. 'I have repeatedly stated that the diagnoses and prescriptions of deceased physicians have always proved in my experience more reliable than those of the living.'

Buckland, William (English geologist and palaeontologist, 1784–1856). Buckland liked to do vivid imitations of pterodactyls in flight during his lectures, while on field trips with his students he dressed with deliberately incongruous formality. He carried with him a mysterious blue bag full of bones.

Burroughs, William S. (American writer, drug fiend, and uxoricide, 1914–97). When the Olympia Press published Burroughs' *The Naked Lunch* in 1959, the *Times Literary Supplement* reviewed it under the headline 'Ugh ... ' There followed a protracted correspondence in the magazine about the worth or otherwise of the book. Edith Sitwell's contribution was to declare 'I do not wish to spend the rest of my life with my nose nailed to other people's lavatories. I prefer Chanel Number 5.'

Burton, Robert (English scholar, 1577–1640). According to Bishop White Kennett, 'The author of *The Anatomy of Melancholy* is said to have laboured long in the writing of this book to suppress his own melancholy, and yet did but improve it; and that some readers have found the same effect. In an interval of vapours he would be extremely pleasant, and raise laughter in any company. Yet I have heard that nothing at last could make him laugh but going down to the Bridge-foot in Oxford, and hearing the barge-men scold and storm and swear at one another, at which he would set his hands to his sides, and laugh most profusely. Yet in his college and chamber so mute and mopish that he was suspected to be *felo de se*.'

Butler, Tom (English bishop, b. 1940). In December 2006, it was alleged that Paul and Nicola Sumpter were sitting in a bar near Southwark Cathedral when they heard their car alarm go off. Rushing outside, they found a grey-haired man in the back seat of the car, throwing the toys of their infant son out of the window. When challenged, the man reportedly said 'I'm the Bishop of Southwark. It's what I do'. He then got out of the car and disappeared into the night, leaving behind a bag containing, among other things, his crucifix.

Button Man, The (English suicide, eighteenth century). The suicide note left by an unfortunate and anonymous man of the eighteenth century read, in its entirety, 'All this buttoning and unbuttoning'.

Byatt, A. S. (English novelist, b. 1936). In this age of declining standards, moral laxity, and a general absence of decorum, it is heartening to know that her children do not presume to call A. S. Byatt 'Mum' or 'Mummy' or 'Mama' or 'Mother' or, God forbid, 'Antonia'. No, A. S. Byatt's children address her, quite properly, as 'A. S. Byatt'.

Byron, George Gordon, Lord (English poet, 1788–1824). Byron had no earlobes.

Byron, William (English baron, 1722–98). The fifth Baron Byron was the great-uncle of the poet Lord Byron. Among his hobbies was the taming and training of crickets. When he died, they departed his estate in a vast swarm.

Cage, Nicolas (American actor, b. 1964). On one of his spending sprees, Cage bought an octopus to keep as a pet. He claimed that studying its movements would enhance his acting skills.

Callaghan, James (English politician and Prime Minister, 1912–2005). When Tom Driberg married Ena Binfield in 1951, Callaghan gave them as a wedding present four ashtrays, two of which were broken.

Cameron, Agnes Deans (Canadian writer and adventurer, 1863–1912). In 1908 Cameron set off on a 10,000-mile round trip from Chicago to the Arctic Ocean. One of the things that struck her on her journey was 'the vicious habit of giving birds bad names'. 'For instance,' she wrote, 'little Robin Red-Breast has successively lived through three tags, *Turdus migratorius, Planesticus migratorius* and *Turdus canadensis*. If he had not been an especially plucky little beggar he would have died under the libels long ago. For my own part I cannot conceive how a man with good red blood in his veins could look a chirky little robin in the eye and call him to his face a *Planesticus migratorius*, when as a chubby youngster he had known the bird and loved him as Robin Red-Breast. One is inclined to ask with suspicion, "Is naming a lost art?"'

Capote, Truman (American writer, real name Truman Streckfus Persons, 1924–84). One of Capote's boyfriends was a dim ex-prison guard and refrigerator repair man named Randy McCuan. One society hostess invited them to dinner under the impression that Capote's lover was the gravel-throated poet and singer Rod McKuen. The evening did not go well.

Cardew, Cornelius (English composer and Marxist-Leninist revolutionary firebrand, 1936–81). In 1966, Cardew was in New York, while his wife Stella remained in London, struggling with four small children and virtually no money in a top-floor flat. Stella wrote a stream of letters to Cardew complaining bitterly about the couple who had come to stay with her. They were helping themselves to food, not paying a penny towards the housekeeping, and leaving Stella to look after their pneumonia-racked child while they went off gallivanting to swish parties. Nor did they show any sign of leaving until Cardew eventually wrote a stern letter ordering them to do so. The names of the couple were Tony Cox and his then wife, the avant-garde Japanese artist Yoko Ono

Carey, Henry (English poet and dramatist, 1687–1743). Apart from writing the words to 'God Save The King', Carey penned the satirical play *Chrononhotonthologos*. It

31

begins with the superb opening line (spoken by Rigdum-Funnidos):

> Aldiborontiphoscophornio! Where left you
> Chrononhotonthologos?

and ends with the stage littered with corpses and the line:

> O horrid! horrible, and horridest horror! Our king!
> our general! our cook! our doctor! All dead! stone
> dead! irrevocably dead! O——h!—— [All groan, a
> tragedy groan.]

The play was so popular in its day that the title entered the language, as a synonym for 'furious, violent, demand-ing, self-centered', appearing in early editions of *Roget's Thesaurus*.

Carr, J. L. (English novelist, 1912–94). Carr liked to carve barbaric stone heads in his back garden. He would wait for them to become weathered and moss-covered, then drive around and conceal them in the long grass in old churchyards to give future historians 'something to think about'.

Caruso, Enrico (Italian tenor, 1873–1921). In 1906, Caruso was arrested and fined ten dollars for 'annoying' respectable ladies in the Monkey House at Central Park Zoo in New York. The fact that the 'annoyances' took place in full view of Knocko the Monkey was considered an aggravating factor in the case. Shortly afterwards, Knocko died of symptoms brought on by 'overexcite-ment'. *See* Garner, Richard Lynch

Casanova, Giacomo Girolamo (Italian adventurer, 1725–98). Prince Charles De Ligne gave this pen-portrait of the ageing Casanova: 'No day passed when there wasn't a quarrel in the house, on account of his coffee, his milk, or a plate of macaroni that he'd asked for. The cook had forgotten his polenta; the head groom had given him a bad coachman . . . dogs had barked in the night; the Count had invited so many guests that he had to eat at a little side table. A hunting horn had shattered his ears with piercing discords. A priest had bored him in trying to convert him. The Count had not greeted him first, before the rest. The soup had been served too hot, maliciously. A servant had made him wait for a drink. He had not been presented to an important gentleman . . . The Count had lent a book without telling him. A groom had not raised his hat in passing. He had spoken German and no one had understood him . . . He is angry – they laugh. He shows some of his own Italian poetry – they laugh. On entering a room he bows as Marcel the famous dancing master had taught him sixty years back – they laugh. At every ball he most gravely dances the minuet – they laugh. He puts on his white plumed hat, his suit of embroidered silk, his black velvet waistcoat, his garters with the strass buckles, his silk stockings – they laugh.'

Casement, Roger (Irish nationalist, 1864–1916). When Casement was serving as British consul in the Congo in 1903, his meals were prepared by a cook known as 'Hairy Bill'. Casement noted in his diary 'Chicken, chicken, custard, custard. . . every day. . . Goddam'.

Cash, Edwin (English publican and mountebank, twentieth century). In the early 1920s, Cash, who owned land

33

in Essex, announced that he had discovered 'magic water' in a well (Well No. 5) at Vange. He bottled the water – high in sulphur content – and marketed it as 'Farmer Cash's Famous Medicinal Vange Water', a cure for nervous disorders, rheumatoid complaints, and lumbago. The business collapsed after a few years when a tuberculosis sanatorium opened on higher ground nearby, the drainage from which contaminated – and removed the magic from – Cash's water. Vange Well No. 5 can still be seen today, a crumbling ruin, in the parish of Fobbing.

Chadwick, Len (English outdoorsman, 1915–88). As 'Fellwalker', Chadwick wrote a regular weekly column in the *Oldham Evening Chronicle* during the 1960s and 70s. He walked thirty to forty miles a day at a cracking pace, often accompanied by young boys to whom he would deliver lectures in Esperanto on a variety of topics.

Chalmers, Thomas (Scottish clergyman and theologian, 1780–1847). Chalmers was deeply devout, and he had no fear of death, because, he said, 'I am of more value than many sparrows.'

Chamberlain, Neville (English politician and Prime Minister, 1869–1940). In 1916, Lloyd George appointed Chamberlain as the Minister for National Service. He sacked him a few months later, having taken a dislike to Chamberlain because 'he had the wrong-shaped head'.

Charles I (English king, 1600–49). According to John Selden in his *Table-Talk*, during Charles's reign, there was 'nothing but Trenchmore & the Cushion dance, Omnium gatherum, tolly polly, hoyte come toyte'. *See* Douglas, Norman

Chekhov, Anton (Russian writer, 1860–1904). In 1890, after a trip to the Far East, Chekhov brought home a pair of mongooses. He described them as 'a mix of rat and crocodile, tiger and monkey', and was vastly amused to watch them urinate in the hats of his visitors, and make off with their galoshes.

Chesterton, G. K. (English writer, 1874–1936). Chesterton explained the proper way to draw a cow: 'When a cow came slouching by in the field next to me, a mere artist might have drawn it; but I always get wrong in the hind legs of quadrupeds. So I drew the soul of the cow; which I saw there plainly walking before me in the sunlight; and the soul was all purple and silver, and had seven horns and the mystery that belongs to all the beasts.' *See* Crowsley, Liz

Christ, Jesus (Son of God, 1–33; also a puppet.) Just as Bernard Levin (q.v.) can refer either to the writer or to the refrigerator of the same name, so Jesus Christ may allude to the Messiah or to his puppet. According to *Puppet Revelation*, the latter Jesus is a 'big mouth' religious puppet – akin to one of Jim Henson's Muppets – perfect for children's church services and puppet ministry. It is fully functional for the teaching of Bible lessons, and with the feature of removable legs, can be used as either a full or half puppet. Made with Christian love and care, the Jesus puppet depicts Christ as loving, kind, and approachable. He wears sandals on his removable legs, and is dressed in a red satin shawl to symbolise the blood he shed for us on the cross. All of his clothing is easily removable. He can be entered through the back, like a ventriloquist's puppet, or up his bottom, when used as a half-body puppet. A plastic attachment is available to make the puppet appear to walk on water. All in all, Jesus is a very affordable puppet for ministries on a limited budget.

Clapton, Eric (English musician, b. 1945). Eric Clapton is an anagram of Narcoleptic.

Clark, Lewis Gaylord (American editor, 1808–73). Editor of *The Knickerbocker*, Clark conducted a vituperative war of words with his rival magazine editor Edgar Allan Poe (q.v.), whom he described as 'a mortified but impotent *littérateur*. . . an ambitious "authorling" perhaps of a small volume of effete and lamentable trash'.

C. L. S. (English letter-writer, nineteenth century). A correspondent known only as C. L. S. had the following letter published in *The Times* on 16 August 1871: 'Sir, – On Monday last I had the misfortune of taking a trip per steamer to Margate. The sea was rough, the ship crowded, and therefore most of the Cockney excursionists prostrate with sea-sickness. On landing on Margate pier I must confess I thought that, instead of landing in an English seaport, I had been transported by magic to a land inhabited by savages and lunatics. The scene that ensued when the unhappy passengers had to pass between the double line of a Margate mob on the pier must be seen to be believed possible in a civilized country. Shouts, yells, howls of delight greeted every pale-looking passenger, as he or she got on the pier, accompanied by a running comment of the lowest, foulest language imaginable. But the most insulted victims were a young lady, who, having had a fit of hysterics on board, had to be assisted up the steps, and a venerable-looking old gentleman with a long grey beard, who, by-the-by, was not sick at all, but being crippled and very old, feebly tottered up the slippery steps leaning on two sticks. "Here's a guy!" "Hallo! You old thief, you won't get drowned, because you know that you are to be hung," etc., and worse than that, were the greetings of that poor old man. All this while a very much silver-bestriped policeman stood calmly by, without interfering by word or deed; and myself, having several ladies to take care of, could do nothing except telling the ruffianly mob some hard words, with, of course, no other effect than to draw all the abuse on myself. This is not an exceptional exhibition of Margate ruffianism, but, as I have been told, is of daily occurrence, only varying in intensity with the roughness of the sea. Public exposure is the only likely thing to put a stop to such ruffianism; and now it is no longer a wonder to me why so many people are ashamed of confessing that they have been to Margate.'

Coleridge, Samuel Taylor (English writer, 1772–1834). Samuel Rogers' *Table-Talk* gave this glimpse of Coleridge (and Wordsworth): 'Coleridge was a marvellous talker . . . Wordsworth and I called upon him one forenoon, when he was in a lodging off Pall Mall. He talked uninterruptedly for about two hours, during which Wordsworth listened to him with profound attention, every now and then nodding his head as if in assent. On quitting the lodging, I said to Wordsworth, "Well, for my own part, I could not make head or tail of Coleridge's oration: pray, did you understand it?" "Not one syllable of it," was Wordsworth's reply.'

Collins, Hal (Maori artist and musician, aka Te Akau, d. 1929). When Peter Warlock (q.v.) was living in a sort of commune at Eynsford in Kent, Collins acted as the household factotum. He subsisted chiefly on gargantuan quantities of stout, and when particularly drunk performed Maori war dances with 'terrifying realism'. He was a talented artist in woodcut and an excellent self-taught pianist. He composed an opera based on *Tristram Shandy*.

Collins, Wilkie (English writer, 1824–89). Shortly after the publication of *The Woman In White* (1859), Collins received a letter from a reader: 'The great failure of your book is your villain. Excuse me if I say, you really do not know a villain. Your Count Fosco is a very poor one, and when next you want a character of that description, I trust you will not disdain to come to me. I know a villain, and have one in my eye at this moment that would far eclipse anything that I have read of in books. Don't think that I am drawing upon my imagination. The man is alive and constantly under my gaze. *In fact he is my own husband.*' The letter was written by the wife of Sir Edward Bulwer-Lytton.

Colman, Ronald (English actor, 1891–1958). Along with Errol Flynn and David Niven, Colman was one of the Hollywood stars who popularised the pencil-thin moustache. Yet according to the film director Henry King, at his screen test for his first big role, as Captain Giovanni Severini in *The White Sister* (1923), Colman confessed: 'I had an injury during the war. A piece of shrapnel hit me in the lip and I cannot grow a moustache.' King assured him that he could pencil in a convincing one, he got the part, and his screen career took off.

Colonel, The Muffin (Suicidal lieutenant colonel, eighteenth century). Thomas De Quincey noted that 'The less variety there is at that meal [breakfast], the more is the danger from any single luxury; and there is one, known by the name of "muffins", which has repeatedly manifested itself to be a plain and direct bounty upon suicide. Darwin, in his *Zoonomia*, reports a case where an officer, holding the rank of lieutenant-colonel, could not tolerate a breakfast in which this odious article was wanting; but, as a savage retribution invariably supervened within an hour or two upon this act of insane sensuality, he came to a resolution that life was intolerable *with* muffins, but still more intolerable *without* muffins. He would stand the nuisance no longer; but yet, being a just man, he would give nature one final chance of reforming her dyspeptic atrocities. Muffins, therefore, being laid at one angle of the breakfast-table, and loaded pistols at another, with rigid equity the Colonel awaited the result. This was naturally pretty much as usual: and then, the poor man, incapable of retreating from his word of honour, committed suicide, having previously left a line for posterity to the effect (though I forget the expression), "That a muffinless world was no world for him: better no life at all than a life dismantled of muffins."'

Conolly, John (English physician, 1794–1866). According to John Timbs, in *Things Not Generally Known* (1859), 'In a lecture delivered at the Royal Institution, Dr Conolly, of the Hanwell Lunatic Asylum, speaking of the moral treatment of the insane, stated as the result of the experience of his whole life, that distorted views on religious subjects are the cause of at least two-thirds of the cases of mania in ladies, especially those belonging to the upper classes.

Touching with all reverence on the proper study of religious books, Dr Conolly lamented that morbid brooding over subjects of theology and points of doctrine is such a fruitful cause of mental diseases. . . Dr Conolly's remarks pointed generally to the impropriety and danger of persons – ladies especially – abandoning themselves to self-guidance, and over-prolonged contemplation on subjects of religious controversy.'

Coolidge, Calvin (American politician and POTUS, 1872–1933). Coolidge's favourite leisure activities were riding a mechanical horse and, when walking the city streets, to pause and gaze at his reflection in plate-glass windows.

Cooper, James Fenimore (American writer, 1789–1851). In 1840, Fenimore Cooper proposed to exhibit, in a touring show of the United States, 'a typical example of an enterprising British lad'. This was 'Boy Jones', briefly notorious in mid-century for his nocturnal incursions into Buckingham Palace. Often covered in soot, Jones – who was described as 'not quite right in his head' – was not discouraged by spells in prison for his offence, and repeatedly entered the palace either through unfastened windows or by climbing down a chimney. He sat on a throne and stole cake from Queen Victoria's larder. His mother refused to allow Cooper to take her son away to America, but his exploits were eventually ended when magistrates had him impressed into the navy and put on board HMS *Warspite* as a deckhand.

Cowell, Simon (English impresario, b. 1959). Cowell worked as a factotum and dogsbody on Stanley Kubrick's

1980 film *The Shining*. One of his jobs was to polish to a gleam the axe wielded by Jack Nicholson.

Cowley, Sir John Guise (Army officer, 1905–93). Cowley was born in the foothills of the Himalayas during an earthquake. His parents shortly afterwards returned to England by ship, aboard which Cowley won an 'ugliest baby' competition. Back home in Dorset, Thomas Hardy was a neighbour. He attended the village church services given by Cowley's father, the rector, and always asked him to read *1 Kings 19*, where Elijah has a vision of an earthquake.

Cradock, Fanny (English cook, real name Phyllis Nan Sortain Pechey, 1909–94). On a continental jaunt, driving along in the 'Duchess', their Bentley Flying Spur, Fanny Cradock and her husband Johnnie were attacked by a flock of enraged owls, nearly causing a terrible accident.

Crandon, Mina (American spiritualist medium, 1888–1941). Mina Crandon, known as 'Margery', was one of the most versatile spirit mediums, able to produce a huge variety of phenomena. She was particularly noted for her 'psychic gloves'. She made her ectoplasm out of the lung tissue of unidentified animals. Houdini pronounced her a charlatan; Conan Doyle raved in her support.

Cravan, Arthur (Swiss Dadaist boxer, real name Fabian Avenarius Lloyd, 1887–vanished 1918). The nephew of Oscar Wilde, Cravan was by turns a poet, professor, boxer, dandy, flâneur, forger, critic, sailor, prospector, card sharper, lumberjack, bricoleur, thief, editor, and chauffeur. He was briefly the world light heavyweight champion, although most of his boxing bouts were undertaken as Dadaist performance art. He and his wife Mina Loy had two imaginary children made of paper, named Gaga and Moche.

Creevey, Thomas (English politician, 1768–1838). Creevey is remembered for his *Papers*, a collection of his journals and correspondence published in 1903, painting a vivid picture of late Georgian England. In one note, in the first year of Victoria's reign, he wrote 'the Queen is a resolute little tit'.

Crowley, Aleister (English occultist, 1875–1947). When young, having heard the adage that a cat has nine lives, Crowley deduced that it would be virtually impossible to kill one. He caught a cat, and by turns poisoned it with a large dose of arsenic, chloroformed it, gassed it, stabbed it, cut its throat, smashed its skull, burned it, drowned it, and then threw it out of the window so 'the fall might remove the ninth life'. He thus proved to himself that it was scientifically possible to kill a cat – though he was 'genuinely sorry for the animal'. In London in 1900, Crowley's rubber mackintosh unaccountably burst into flames, and on five occasions horses bolted at the sight of him.

Crowsley, Liz (English veterinarian, 1960–2009). Crowsley was murdered by cows in a field in the Yorkshire Dales. A local resident, Mrs Johnson, heard 'an unusual bellow' and found the dead body of the veterinarian leaning against a stone wall, with the cows 'all stood, huddled together in an arch' around her. *See* Davies, Marion

Cruse, A. J. (English phillumenist, dates unknown). In his 1946 book *Matchbox Labels Of The World, With a History of Fire-Making Appliances from Primitive Man to the Modern Match, together with a History of the World's Labels*, Cruse made some pointed remarks about foreign, non-British matches and matchboxes. 'France still produces abominable sulphurous State-made matches. The label designs are sometimes poor and the colouring crude', he wrote. Cruse added: 'One of the earliest German labels, issued in 1835, illustrates, by drawing, how to ignite the match by rubbing it on the box. Even the most ignorant person knew how to light a match, and the label appears a very futile one.'

Cuif-Rimbaud, Vitalie (French poet's mother, 1825–1907). In 1906, Mme. Rimbaud wrote to her daughter: 'I am not writing to wish you a Good New Year. It's futile. Actions are everything.' *See* Hitchens, Peter

Cutler, Ivor (Scottish writer, musician, and performer, 1923–2006). Cutler served in the RAF during the Second World War, where he alarmed his superiors by gazing dreamily at clouds rather than navigating the planes he flew in. Later, as a London teacher, he equally alarmed parents by getting the children in his drama classes to roleplay the killing of their siblings. His cluttered flat in north London contained a set of ivory cutlery and a wax ear hammered into the wall with six-inch nails.

Cuvier, Georges (French naturalist, 1769–1832). Cuvier's dying words were: 'It was I who discovered leeches have red blood!'

Damian, John (Italian alchemist, sixteenth century). Giovanni Damiano de Falcucci was an alchemist at the court of King James IV of Scotland, where he was known as 'John Damian' or 'the French Leech'. In addition to the usual alchemical activity of transmuting base metal into gold, he organised dances and other entertainments and, in 1507, made an attempt to fly to France from the battlements of Stirling castle. The result of this escapade was a broken thigh. Damian attributed his failure to the presence of too many hen's feathers in his flying-suit of eagle feathers.

Darger, Henry (American janitor, writer, and artist, 1892–1973). Darger was a recluse who worked as a janitor and lived in a single room in a Chicago boarding house. For decades he devoted himself to his novel, *The Story of the Vivian Girls, in What is Known as the Realms of the Unreal, of the Glandeco-Angelinian War Storm, Caused by the Child Slave Rebellion.* It runs to 15,145 closely-typed pages and is illustrated with large, frieze-like watercolours and collages. His landlords discovered his work shortly before his death, when he had moved to a Catholic hospice. Darger also found time to write another novel (more than 10,000 pages) and an autobiography (almost 5,000 pages), to keep a daily weather record, and to attend Catholic Mass, sometimes as many as five times per day.

D'Arrigo, Angelo (French-Sicilian ornithologist and aviator, 1961–2006). D'Arrigo obtained two Andean condor eggs from an Austrian university and determined to act as the unhatched birds' 'mother', without whom they might not learn to fly. Depositing the eggs in a nest at his aviary on the slopes of Mount Etna, he spoke to them daily to get the chicks inside used to the sound of his voice. Similarly, when they hatched, he covered the nest with a black and white hang-glider, shaped like a condor, to accustom them to its shape and presence. He took trips in the glider and came back with food for the chicks, and also gave them flying lessons. Sadly, he was killed in a light aircraft crash (in which he was a passenger) before he was able to return the condors to the Andes.

Darwin, Charles (English naturalist, 1809–82). Had Robert FitzRoy, the captain of HMS *Beagle*, followed his instincts, the history of science could have changed utterly. As Darwin recorded in his autobiography: 'Next day I started for Cambridge to see Henslow, and thence to London to see FitzRoy, and all was soon arranged. Afterwards, on becoming  very intimate with FitzRoy, I heard that I had run a very narrow risk of being rejected, on account of the shape of my nose! He was an ardent disciple of Lavater, and was convinced that he could judge of a man's character by the outline of his features; and he doubted whether any one with my nose could possess sufficient energy and determination for the voyage. But I think he was afterwards well satisfied that my nose had spoken falsely.'

Davies, Marion (American actress, 1897–1961). Marion Davies was frightened of cows. In one of her early films, she was required to milk a cow, or at least to pretend to do so. As she approached it, however, the cow mooed and kicked over the milking-pail, causing the actress to run away, jumping over a fence and hiding behind a bush. Unable to find her, the crew used a stand-in and shot her from behind. 'I was shaking all day long, I was so frightened,' wrote Davies. Later, on a trip to Germany with William Randolph Hearst, she sulked and refused to speak for two days because she missed the chance to meet Adolf Hitler. *See* Gladstone, William Ewart

Davies, Peter Maxwell (English composer, b. 1934). In 2005, Davies was cautioned by the police for having the remains of a whooper swan in his possession. He claimed to have found the swan dead, electrocuted by a power line, and to have taken it to his Orkney home to make a terrine of it and to donate the wings to the local primary school so they could be used as props in a nativity play. He had not considered that swans are a protected species, although he did contact the local office of the Royal Society For The Protection Of Birds, whose spokesman said: 'He doesn't have to ring us to report dead swans, but

I enjoy hearing from him because he's always good value.'
See Henman, Tim

Davis, John (English explorer, *c.* 1550–1605). The man who discovered the Falkland Isles made three Arctic voyages between 1585 and 1587. In order to befriend the Eskimos, he took with him a small band of musicians to charm them with English folk tunes. As Admiral Sir Edward Evans wrote, 'What fun it must have been to see his mariners and himself dancing in the summer snows, and on the harder palaeozoic rocks and jet-black and green slates, which must have shaken with their bear-like prancings!' Davis also took wrestlers and athletes along, to put on displays for the natives.

Day, Thomas (English writer, 1748–89). In order to find the perfect wife, Day – a devotee of the educational theories of Jean-Jacques Rousseau – removed two girls from a foundling's hospital, fled with them to France, and trained them to become his ideal. One, named Sabrina, seemed promising, and he brought her back to England to complete her education. However, she failed various tests. When Day dripped hot sealing wax on her arm, she screamed, and when he fired a revolver close by, she was startled. After concluding that she was not sufficiently phlegmatic, he paid her off with an allowance and never saw her again.

Day-Lewis, Daniel (English actor, b. 1957). At the turn of the century Day-Lewis took a sabbatical from the film business and spent five years living in Florence and working as an apprentice to master cobbler Stefano Berner. He later trained as a carpenter, and his then nine-year-old son did not realise his father was an actor, but thought he worked full-time on a building site.

De André, Fabrizio (Italian singer-songwriter, 1940–99). De André's first wife's given name was Puny. In 1979 he was kidnapped by Sardinian bandits, and released after payment of a ransom. His first album was called *Volume One*, and his third was called *Volume Three*. In between, he released a second album called, not *Volume Two*, but *Tutti morimmo a stento* ('We all died agonizingly').

De Bury, Richard (English bishop, writer, and book-collector, 1287–1345). In his *Philobiblon*, De Bury complained about those who mistreat books: 'His nails are stuffed with filth as black as jet, with which he marks any passage that pleases him. He distributes a multitude of straws, which he inserts to stick out in different places, so that the halm may remind him of what his memory cannot retain. He does not fear to eat fruit or cheese over an open book, or carelessly to carry a cup to and from his mouth; and because he has no wallet at hand he drops into books the fragments that are left. Aye, and then hastily folding his arms he leans forward on the book, and by a brief spell of study invites a prolonged nap; and then, by way of mending the wrinkles, he folds back the margin of the leaves. Now the rain is over and gone, and the flowers have appeared in our land. Then the scholar we are speaking of will stuff his volume with violets and primroses, with roses and quatrefoil. Then he will use his wet and perspiring hands to turn over the volumes; then he will thump the white vellum with gloves covered with all kinds of dust . . . then at the sting of the biting flea the sacred book is flung aside, and is hardly shut for another month, until it is so full of the dust that has found its way within, that it resists the effort to close it.'

De Chasseneuz, Barthélemy (French jurist, 1480–1541). De Chasseneuz devised the precise wording for the excommunication and banishment of snails, flies, mice, moles, ants, caterpillars, and so on. 'O snails, caterpillars, and other obscene creatures, which destroy the food of our neighbours, depart hence! Leave these cantons which you are devastating, and take refuge in those localities where you can injure no one! In Nomine Patris &c.'

De Clifford, Nerea (English cat lover, 1905–87). Nerea de Clifford was the author of the pamphlet 'What British Cats Think About Television', in which she noted 'most cats show an interest of some kind, though it is often of hostility. . . a significant reaction is the display of excitement when any picture, especially of birds, moves quickly across the screen'.

De Gaulle, Yvonne (French First Lady, 1900–79). At a formal dinner in the British Embassy in Paris shortly after the war, Madame De Gaulle was asked what she was looking forward to now that her husband had left office. 'A penis', she replied, at which point the General gently corrected her. 'No, my dear, you are mispronouncing the word. In English they say "'appiness".'

Delacroix, Eugène (French artist, 1798–1863). Delacroix believed that in order to guarantee a long life, only two things were necessary. First, one must get up very early in the mornings. Second, above all and *most important,* once awake one must avoid dozing off again. *See* Boorde, Andrew

Della, Alice (English? mystery woman, nineteenth century). Alice Della placed an advertisement in *The Young Englishman* on 29 April 1876: 'To The Curious – Ladies and gentlemen, send three stamps to Miss Alice Della, 22 Chatham-road, Camberwell, London, and you will receive 3 things that will greatly surprise and astonish you. Sent, by return of post.'

Dellschau, Charles (Prussian-American butcher and artist, 1830–1923). Dellschau was an outsider artist who made mixed-media pictures of fantastic flying machines. These were intended as working blueprints produced for a California secret society named the Sonora Aero Club. Active in the 1850s, the club claimed to have created an anti-gravity fuel named NB Gas, made from a green crystal called Supe distilled from coal, to which water was added.

DeMille, Cecil B. (American film director and producer, 1881–1959). DeMille refused to touch used currency and would send his secretary to the bank several times a day to replace old notes with fresh new ones. He always addressed actress Gloria Swanson as 'Young Fellow'.

De Quincey, Thomas (English writer, 1785–1859). De Quincey kept in his study a large bathtub that he used as a 'reservoir' for his papers. It was filled to the brim with 'every paper written *by* me, *to* me, *for* me, *of* or *concerning* me and, finally, *against* me'. Asked at short notice to provide an article for *The Athenaeum* magazine, De Quincey had the bright idea of plucking an already-written piece at random from the tub. To make the selection, he dressed his son in a potato-sack, with holes cut through the bottom for his legs, tied with 'distressing tightness about his throat, leaving only a loophole for his right arm to play freely'. The child dipped five times into the pile at De Quincey's bidding. The first paper was an unopened dinner invitation. The second and third were demands from creditors. The fourth was the text of a lecture delivered to De Quincey by one of his friends on the perils of procrastination. The fifth and final piece of paper was blank.

De Southchurch, Richard (English sheriff, d. 1294). De Southchurch hatched an innovatory scheme to quell a rebellion against King Henry III in 1267. While levying requisitions from the villagers of Chafford Hundred, including 'oats and wheat, of bacon, beef, cheese and pease; of chickens to feed the wounded and tow and eggs to make dressings for their wounds and linen for bandages, of chord to make ropes for the catapults, of picks and calthrops and spades to lay low the walls of London', he added 'cocks, forty and more, to whose feet he declared he would tie fire, and send them flying into London to burn it down'. This is thought to be the first instance in English history of the planned use of incendiary dive-bombing poultry birds.

De Worde, Wynkyn (German-English printer and publisher, d. 1534). In 1508 Wynkyn De Worde printed *The Booke Of Kervinge*, which includes a helpful list of the terms used for carving different types of meat, poultry, birds, and fish: 'The terms of a carver be as here

51

followeth. Break that deer – lesche (leach) that brawn – rear that goose – lift that swan – sauce that capon – spoil that hen – frusche (fruss) that chicken – unbrace that mallard – unlace that coney – dismember that heron – display that crane – disfigure that peacock – unjoint that bittern – untache that curlew – alaye that felande – wing that partridge – wing that quail – mine that plover – thigh that pigeon – border that pasty – thigh that woodcock – thigh all manner small birds – timber that fire – tire that egg – chine that salmon – string that lamprey – splat that pike – sauce that plaice – sauce that tench – splay that bream – side that haddock – tusk that barbel – culpon that trout – fin that chevin – trassene that eel – tranch that sturgeon – undertranch that porpoise – tame that crab – barb that lobster. Here endeth the goodly terms of Carving.'

Dickens, Charles (English novelist, 1812–70). Dickens' handwriting was minute, and he had a habit of writing with blue ink on blue paper.

Dickinson, Emily (American poet, 1830–86). Emily Dickinson held the view that people must have puddings. She expressed this, very tentatively and suggestively, to Thomas Wentworth Higginson, as if puddings 'were meteors or comets'.

Dingwall, Eric (English psychic researcher, 1890–1986). Dingwall gave a glimpse of the exciting life of a psychic researcher in his account of a séance conducted by the medium Stella C. 'When the red light was switched on under the table, I lay down on the floor and looked through the passage towards the luminous screen. From near the medium's foot, which was invisible, I saw an egg-shaped body beginning to crawl towards the centre of the floor under the table. It was white, and where the light was reflected it appeared opal. To the end nearest the medium was attached a thin white neck like a piece of macaroni. It advanced towards the centre and then rapidly withdrew to the shadow.' Quite what eldritch forces were being communed with remains unexplained.

Dobson (English miller, seventeenth century). Dobson was a miller of Charlton in Kent. He was so excited by the return from exile of King Charles II that he burned down his own windmill in joyous celebration. *See* William I

Donaldson, William (English writer, 1935–2005). The author of the Henry Root letters was, in the 1960s, a theatrical impresario. One of his shows involved a Red Indian troupe, a fire-eater, a woman with an enormous snake, a formidable singer called Ida Barr, a Polish boxer who challenged members of the audience to fight him, Demetrius the Gladiator whose act involved blowing up hot-water bottles, a man called Bob who hit himself on the head with a tin tray while singing *Mule Train*, and an outrageous, alcoholic, drag act called Mrs Shufflewick.

Donisthorpe, Horace St. John Kelly (English coleopterist and myrmecologist, 1870–1951). Donisthorpe had a passion for ants, and wrote more than 800 books and papers on the subject. After his death, R. W. Lloyd wrote an appreciation of him in the *Entomologist's Monthly Magazine*: 'Mr Donisthorpe was a very fine Coleopterist, but he had that curious "kink" shared by one or two other people, that he would only put in his collection beetles he had taken with his own hands. Luckily for him he was a man of leisure and he was able to go about the country when he heard of any rare beetles being taken. It led, however, to some curious results, as on a celebrated occasion when a collector in the New Forest got a very rare beetle – Velleius I believe it was – and advised Mr Donisthorpe, who telegraphed him to put a tumbler over it on the ground and keep it there until he was able to go and collect it himself.'

Donnelly, Ignatius (American politician and writer, 1831–1901). With his 1882 book *Atlantis: The Antediluvian World*, Donnelly single-handedly popularised the idea of the submerged lost civilisation. William Gladstone (q.v.) found the book so persuasive that he attempted to get government funding for an expedition to locate Atlantis – his request was turned down. (Gladstone, incidentally, concluded that all Ancient Greeks were colour-blind, based on the paucity of colour-words in the writings of Homer.) One of Donnelly's other enthusiasms was the 'true' authorship of the plays of Shakespeare, expounded at inordinate length in *The Great Cryptogram* (1888). This demonstrated that the canon is cram-packed with codes and ciphers identifying Francis Bacon as the real author. Donnelly's methods have been employed by later conspiracy theorists, finding similar deeply-hidden codes in the Bible and in Melville's *Moby-Dick*.

Dorfeuille, Joseph (French-American mountebank, d. 1840). 'Dorfeuille's Hell', a chamber of horrors museum in Cincinnati, was immortalised by Fanny Trollope in *Domestic Manners Of The Americans*: 'He has constructed a pandaemonium in an upper story of his museum, in which he has congregated all the images of horror that his fertile fancy could devise; dwarfs that by machinery grow into giants before the eyes of the spectator; imps of ebony with eyes of flame; monstrous reptiles devouring youth and beauty; lakes of fire, and mountains of ice; in short, wax, paint and springs have done wonders. To give the scheme some more effect, he makes it visible only through a grate of massive iron bars, among which are arranged wires connected with an electrical machine in a neighbouring chamber; should any daring hand or foot obtrude itself with the bars, it receives a smart shock, that often passes through many of the crowd, and the cause being unknown, the effect is exceedingly comic; terror, astonishment, curiosity, are all set in action, and all contribute to make "Dorfeuille's Hell" one of the most amusing exhibitions imaginable.'

Douglas, Norman (English writer, 1868–1952). The much-travelled Douglas carried everywhere with him a small, hard pillow which he called Alfred. *See* Sheldon, May French

Doyle, Sir Arthur Conan (Scottish writer, 1859–1930). Conan Doyle devised a foolproof method of dealing with a rampaging rhinoceros. Accompanied by his two sons in East Africa, he suggested that they walk towards any such rhinoceros in a line, with himself in the centre and the boys flanking him. Naturally, the beast would charge towards Conan Doyle, whereupon he would startle it by opening his umbrella. As it paused in consternation, the boys could shoot it from either side. They were not attacked by a rhinoceros, so the writer was unable to test the efficacy of his method.

Duchamp, Marcel (French artist, 1887–1968) *See* Freytag-Loringhoven, Elsa von

Ducrow, Andrew (English circus performer, 1793–1842). Ducrow was a showman, 'the Colossus of Equestrians', who wrestled with lions, re-enacted scenes from Napoleonic battles, and could lift four or five children using nothing more than his teeth. His tomb in Kensal Green cemetery, an Egyptian extravaganza, was described by *The Builder* magazine as 'ponderous coxcombry'.

Dufour (French magician, nineteenth century). Harry Houdini described a typical repast *chez* Dufour: 'The dinner began with a soup of asps in simmering oil. On each side was a dish of vegetables, one containing thistles and burdocks, and the other fuming acid. Other side dishes, of turtles, rats, bats and moles, were garnished with live coals. For the fish course he ate a dish of snakes in boiling tar and pitch. His roast was a screech owl in a sauce of glowing brimstone. The salad proved to be spider webs full of small explosive squibs, a plate of butterfly wings and manna worms, a dish of toads surrounded with flies, crickets, grasshoppers, church beetles, spiders, and caterpillars. He washed all this down with flaming brandy, and for dessert ate the four large candles standing on the table, both of the hanging side lamps with their contents, and finally the large center lamp, oil, wick and all. This leaving the room in darkness, Dufour's face shone out in a mask of living flames.' *See* Southey, Robert

Duncan, Isadora (American dancer, 1877–1927). Isadora Duncan built a temple in Greece where she intended to 'greet the rising sun with joyous songs and dances'. Later she became an enthusiastic Bolshevik in Moscow and took hundreds of working-class children under her wing, teaching them to enact the endurance of the proletariat through the medium of dance. One contemporary critic described her own performances: 'All she did was stand, taking at times a few steps from one side to the other, or stoop, while she looked up and raised her arms above her head.'

Durham, Carl T. (American politician, 1892–1974). Long before the kerfuffle over the Danish cartoons of the Prophet Mohammed, Durham sparked a row regarding a cartoon of Adam and Eve in an official US government publication. The Congressman and his House Military Affairs subcommittee were worried that the first man and woman were shown to have navels, which was clearly unBiblical and possibly part of a Communist plot.

Eddy, Mary Baker (American Christian Scientist, 1821–1910). Mary Baker Eddy was convinced that one of her three husbands had been murdered by something called 'mesmeric poison'. When travelling on the railways, she insisted that an extra engine go ahead of her own train in order to drive away any 'malicious animal magnetism' lying in wait.

Edgerly, Webster (American social reformer, lawyer, and writer, 1852–1926). When not writing tracts on euthanasia, healthy diet, and the power of personal magnetism, Edgerly turned his hand to the theatre. In 1890 he brought his play *Christopher Columbus, or The Discovery of America* to New York. The *New York Times* reported: 'Mr. Edgerly wrote his play especially for Mr. Shaftesbury, he declares. This is not astonishing when it is known that Edgerly and Shaftesbury are one and the same person. By combining the two functions of actor and author, Christopher Columbus becomes, in the hands of Mr. Edgerly, a portly individual of uncertain age, who struts up and down the stage spouting the most extraordinary balderdash that ever fell from mortal lips. In his endeavours to prove to the Spanish Junta that the world is round Columbus uses an every-day school globe, with a map of the American continent clearly painted on its surface. And yet with such evidence as this he cannot carry his point.'

Edwards, Jill (American writer, twentieth century). In her 1950 book *Personality Pointers*, Jill Edwards listed some of the questions one should ask oneself each day: 'Do I know what my colours are? Do I make my vowels sing? Am I direct, sincere and simple? Do I know the proper way to sit in and rise from a chair? Am I lovable? Am I original? Am I valiant? Have I made a legal will? Do I know where it is? Do I hang up my clothes as soon as I take them off? Do I sew a snap-fastener on to each end of a piece of tape about an inch and a half long, and sew these tapes in the centre of all shoulder seams? Am I so poised, so on my centre, so innately joyous that life cannot sway me this way or that?'

Egerton, Francis, 8th Earl of Bridgewater (English dog-lover, 1756–1829). Egerton kept his local bootmaker gainfully employed, as he wore a brand new pair of boots every day. Those he had worn he lined up in a row to mark the passing of the year. He also had boots specially made for his dogs, a dozen of which dined with him each day, dressed in livery, with napkins tied around their necks, sat on chairs, with servants stationed behind them. Ill-behaved dogs were banished to an antechamber on the following day, though they still received the same sumptuous meals.

Eliot, George (English writer, real name Mary Ann Evans, 1819–80). George Eliot once had her head shaved in the

interests of pseudo-science, so that a phrenologist could examine her 'bumps' without hindrance.

Eliot, John (English writer, sixteenth century). In his 1593 book *Ortho-epia Gallica*, Eliot coined the word *dezink-hornifistibulated*. He wrote: 'I retired myselfe among the merrie muses, and by the worke of my pen and inke, have dezinkhornifistibulated a fantasticall Rapsody of dia-logisme, to the end that I would not be found an idle drone among so many famous teachers and professors of noble languages.' Sadly, nobody has seen fit to use the word ever since.

Eliot, T. S. (American poet, 1888–1965). In the early 1920s in London, as the strain of his marriage to his unhinged first wife Vivienne took hold, Eliot advertised his predicament by rubbing on to his cheeks a dusting of fine green powder. This was intended to make him look even more careworn than he was, and to evoke sympathy from his friends. Vivienne complained at the time that 'only one human being seemed to interest him, an ex-policeman of about seventy years of age, who acted as odd-job man and was an habitual drunkard'. This 'tortoise-like individual' (who wore a bowler hat indoors) once presented himself at a dinner party attended by James and Nora Joyce. The original title of 'The Waste Land' was 'He Do The Police In Different Voices', which perhaps explains the closeness Eliot felt towards the ex-copper.

Elizabeth I (English queen, 1533–1603). During Elizabeth's reign, 'the verge' was an area of legal jurisdiction defined as the territory within a twelve-mile radius of the body of the Queen, wherever she happened to be.

Elliot, John (English apothecary and scientist, 1747–87). The great astronomer Sir William Herschel believed that the sun was inhabited. He was persuaded by the theories of Elliot, of whom it was written 'he maintained that the light of the sun arose from what he called a dense and universal twilight. He further believed that the sun might be inhabited. When he was brought before the Old Bailey for having occasioned the death of Miss Boydell, his friends maintained that he was mad, and thought they could prove it abundantly by showing the writings wherein the opinions we have just cited were found developed.' The judge agreed, and Elliot was acquitted of murder, but starved himself to death while held in Newgate prison.

Elliot, R. H. (English occultist, twentieth century). Elliot made a long and careful study of snakes. He concluded that all of them were very stupid animals.

Eno, Brian Peter George St. John le Baptiste de la Salle (English 'Brain One', b. 1948). In the 1970s Eno and his cat Eric appeared in adverts for Purina cat food.

Erlik (Siberian God of Darkness). M. A. Czaplicka, in *Shamanism In Siberia*, explained how to deal with Erlik: 'The kam, as if approaching the Yurta of Erlik and coming into his presence, bows, brings his drum up to his forehead, and says, "Mergu! Mergu!" Then he declares whence and why he comes. Suddenly he shouts; this is meant to indicate that Erlik is angry that a mortal should dare to enter his yurta. The frightened kam leaps backward towards the door, but gathers fresh courage and again approaches Erlik's throne. After this performance has been gone through three times, Erlik speaks: "Winged creatures cannot fly hither, beings with bones cannot come: how have you, ill-smelling black beetle, made your way to my abode?" Then the kam stoops and with his drum makes certain movements as if dipping up wine. He presents the wine to Erlik; and makes a shuddering movement like that of one who drinks strong wine, to indicate, that Erlik has drunk. When he perceives that Erlik's humour is somewhat milder he makes him offerings of gifts. Erlik is moved by the offerings of the kam, and promises increase of cattle, declares which mare will foal, and even specifies what marking the young one will have. The kam returns in high spirits, not on his horse as he went, but on a goose.'

Eve (Edenite first woman, 4001 BC–?). In his 1932 book *Evolution And Theology*, the Catholic priest Ernest C. Messenger insisted that the creation of Eve, from Adam's side, was miraculous. 'The formation of Eve *ex Adamo*', he wrote, 'seems to be so clear in Scripture and Tradition that, at the very least, it cannot be prudently called into question. Further, there is no reason to doubt it, other than the difficulty of understanding how it could take place.'

Fabre, J. H. (French entomologist, 1823–1915). In his posthumously published *Social Life In The Insect World* (1923), Fabre claimed that the praying mantis hypnotises its prey by pretending to be a ghost.

Faith, Adam (English singer and actor, real name Terence Nelhams-Wright, 1940–2003). Adam Faith's last words, spoken in a Stoke-on-Trent hotel room immediately prior to his fatal heart attack, were 'Channel Five is shit, isn't it? Christ, the crap they put on there. It's a waste of space.'

Felix, Julie (American folk singer, b. 1938). When her brief period of stardom was on the wane, Julie Felix became a keen advocate of trepanning. She recorded songs including 'Brainbloodvolume' and 'The Great Brain Robbery', drilled a hole in her skull, and encouraged others to do likewise.

Fewkes, Jesse Walter (American anthropologist and folklorist, 1850–1930). It is Fewkes we have to thank for our understanding of Passamaquoddy folklore. Without him, we may not have learned of Kewok, a formless being with icy heart, regarded as a terrible one, of Pedogiic, thunder, of Pesok que tuk, lightning, or of Pook-jin-squess, the

Jug, called also the toad woman. Then there is Glooscap, the beneficent being whose deeds are generally super-human, and who figures in many heroic tales of the Passamaquoddies. The term as applied to a man is one of contempt. To call a man glooscap, or a woman glooscapess, is to call them liars. And let us not forget Chematiquess, the big rabbit.

Field, Eugene (American writer, 1850–95). The author of 'Wynken, Blynken, and Nod', Field had a childhood sweetheart with the captivating name Captivity Waite.

Firbank, Ronald (English novelist, 1886–1926). Chapter XX of Firbank's 1916 novel *Inclinations*, complete and unabridged:

> 'Mabel! Mabel! Mabel! Mabel!
> Mabel! Mabel! Mabel! Mabel!'

Fletcher, Horace (American health food enthusiast, 'the Great Masticator', 1849–1919). To gather data to prove his theory that chewing one's food hundreds and hundreds of times was nutritionally beneficial, Horace Fletcher weighed the daily bodily 'input and output' of himself and 'his man Carl' during a bicycling tour of France. Carl was a young Tyrolean – dressed in national costume – who carried the weighing scale, pushed Fletcher's bicycle up the steeper inclines, and acted as a general factotum. *See* Kafka, Franz

Foote, Samuel (English actor and dramatist, 1720–77). Foote invented the term 'The Great Panjandrum'. The actor Charles Macklin boasted that he could memorise any passage of text at a single reading. Foote wrote, and handed to him, the following:

'So she went into the garden to cut a cabbage-leaf to make an apple-pie; and at the same time a great she-bear, coming up the street, pops its head into the shop. "What! No soap?" So he died, and she very imprudently married the barber; and there were present the Picninnies, and the Joblillies, and the Garyulies, and the grand Panjandrum himself, with the little round button at top, and they all fell to playing the game of catch-as-catch-can till the gunpowder ran out at the heels of their boots.'

Macklin refused to repeat a word of it and stomped off in a huff.

Ford, Ford Madox (English writer, 1873–1939). *The English Review* was one of the most important literary journals of the early twentieth century, publishing writers including Joseph Conrad, D. H. Lawrence, Ezra Pound, and Henry James. Its founder editor, Ford Madox Ford, unable to concentrate due to the constant stream of visitors to his office, did much of the editorial work from a seat in the stalls at the Shepherd's Bush Empire. He dealt with manuscripts and submissions during the duller acts, occasionally looking up to enjoy turns by music hall stars such as Little Tich and Vesta Victoria.

Fossmo, Helge (Swedish pastor, twenty-first century). In 2004, Fossmo, a Lutheran pastor, was jailed for life. He had composed fake text messages from God commanding his lover to murder his wife and the husband of another lover.

Foster, William Trufant (American educator, 1879–1950). In 1914, Foster edited the timely book *The Social Emergency: Studies In Sex Hygiene And Morals*. In his introduction, he lamented that 'Not all of those who have been stimulated by the new freedom of speech to thrust themselves forward as teachers of sex hygiene, and as social reformers, are safe leaders. Some are ignorant and unaware that enthusiasm is not a satisfactory substitute for knowledge. Some are hysterical. At a recent purity convention, a woman said, "I know little about the facts, but it is wonderful how much ignorance can accomplish when accompanied by devotion and persistence." That declaration was applauded.'

Franklin, Sir John (English explorer, 1786–1847). In search of the North-West Passage, Franklin's ships, the *Erebus* and *Terror*, became trapped in ice, and the expedition set out to cross the Canadian Arctic on foot. They left their guns behind, but among the items they carried with them were a set of monogrammed silver cutlery, a backgammon board, a cigar case, a clothes brush, a tin of button polish, and a copy of *The Vicar of Wakefield*. Every member of the party perished.

Frederick, Prince of Wales (English prince, 1707–51). Frederick, heir to the throne who died before he succeeded, was loathed by his parents, George II and Caroline of Ansbach. His mother said of him, 'If I was to see him in hell, I should feel no more for him than I should for any other rogue who ever went there.' For saying as much, she was chided by the king, who thought it far too kind. As far as he was concerned, Prince Frederick was 'a monster and the greatest villain that was ever born'.

Freeman, Alan (Australian disc jockey, 1927–2006). The disc jockey known as 'Fluff' had a short-lived acting career in the 1960s, appearing in the film *Dr Terror's House Of Horrors* among others. Later, he joined the small but distinguished band of actors who have been cast as God, playing the Almighty twice on television. *See* Hardy, G. H.

Freud, Lucian (German-English painter, 1922–2011). One of Freud's favourite snacks was a partridge, torn to pieces and eaten with his bare hands.

Freud, Sigmund (Viennese quack, 1856–1939). Freud and Jung (q.v.) had a falling-out over a mysterious exploding bookcase. Jung reported in his memoirs: 'While Freud was going on this way, I had a curious sensation. It was as if my diaphragm were made of iron and were becoming red-hot – a glowing vault. And at that moment there was such a loud report in the bookcase, which stood right next to us, that we both started up in alarm, fearing the thing was going to topple over on us. I said to Freud: "There, that is an example of a so-called catalytic exteriorization phenomenon." "Oh come," he exclaimed. "That is sheer bosh." "It is not," I replied. "You are mistaken, Herr Professor. And to prove my point I now predict that in a moment there will be another such loud report!" Sure enough, no sooner had I said the words than the same detonation went off in the bookcase. To this day I do not know what gave me this certainty. But I knew beyond all doubt that the report would come again. Freud only stared aghast at me. I do not know what was in his mind, or what his look meant. In any case, this incident aroused his distrust of me, and I had the feeling that I had done something against him. I never afterward discussed the incident with him.'

Freytag-Loringhoven, Elsa von (German Dadaist, 1874–1927). In New York during the First World War, Baroness Elsa von Freytag-Loringhoven became besotted with fellow European expatriate Marcel Duchamp, of whom it was said that 'he could insinuate his hand under a woman's bodice

and hug her very body without it being at all apparent'. The Baroness has been credited with choosing the urinal Duchamp notoriously exhibited in 1917. She liked to dress in a bustle with a tail-light, a brassière made of tin cans and string, a necklace composed of a birdcage with a canary inside, and a French soldier's helmet on her vermilion crewcut. Her poems were first published more than seventy years after her death, in 2011.

Friend, Bob (English journalist, 1938–2008). Friend took great pleasure in imitating the barking of dogs, often in television studios just before news broadcasts. On one occasion in 1963 he was sent to interview the then Home Secretary, Reginald Maudling, at his home. After a few drinks, Friend wandered off into the back garden, climbed a tree, barked like a dog for some time and then fell asleep. He had to be coaxed down at three o'clock in the morning.

Fripp, Robert (English musician, b. 1946). Fripp has expressed the considered view that nobody can play his guitar part to David Bowie's song 'Beauty And The Beast', from the *Heroes* album, without getting an erection.

Fry, Stephen (English tweeter, b. 1957; also a large gorilla made of granite). *See* Brooker, Gary

Fuller, Osgood Eaton (American writer, 1835–1900). In *Brave Men And Women*, Fuller asked: 'What shall we read? Shall our minds be the receptacle of every thing that an author has a mind to write? Shall there be no distinction between the tree of life and the tree of death? Shall we stoop down and drink out of the trough which the wickedness of men has filled with pollution and shame? Shall we mire in impurity, and chase fantastic will-o'-the-wisps across the swamps, when we might walk in the blooming gardens of God? O, no.'

Galgani, Gemma (Italian saint and mystic, 1878–1903). Gemma Galgani's short life was filled with mystic visions of Christ, the Virgin Mary, and the Devil. She managed to fight off the temptations of the latter. Despite suffering from tuberculosis, she was able to levitate, and was occasionally to be found in mid-air, clutching a large crucifix hanging on the wall of her parents' living room, passionately kissing the wound in Christ's side.

Galton, Francis (English polymath, 1822–1911). Galton felt that the worship of idols as practised by certain Africans was the truest kind of religious experience. He obtained a puppet of Mr Punch and forced his mind to believe it possessed divine powers. After some time, he had 'a large share of the feelings a barbarian entertains towards his idol', and could not look at the puppet without an overwhelming emotion of reverence.

Gandhi, Mohandas Karamchand (Indian statesman, 1869–1948). In 1931, Winston Churchill said of Gandhi, 'It is alarming and nauseating to see Mr Gandhi, a seditious Middle Temple lawyer, now posing as a fakir of a type well known in the east, striding half naked up the steps of the viceregal palace'.

Garfunkel, Art (American singer, actor, poet and Renaissance Man, b. 1941). Garfunkel, or 'The G.', as he likes to be known, maintains an online list of every book he has read since 1968.

Garner, Richard Lynch (American zoologist, 1848–1920). Garner taught himself the language of monkeys and had many long conversations with them in their own tongue, which he recorded in his 1892 book *The Speech Of Monkeys. See* Grimaldi, Joseph

Gaudier-Brzeska, Henri (French sculptor, 1891–1915). From the trenches of World War One, Gaudier-Brzeska sent excited letters to his friends extolling the aesthetic beauty of machine guns and other armaments. He was killed in action, by one such gun, in 1915.

Geisel, Theodore (American writer and illustrator, 1904–91). Geisel was enormously successful in the advertising industry. In the 1930s, his work promoting insecticides and motorboat lubricants gave him a public profile before he adopted the pseudonym Dr. Seuss and became a best-selling children's author.

Geller, Uri (Israeli conjurer, b. 1946). In 2002 Geller was a participant in the television programme *I'm A*

Celebrity. . . Get Me Out Of Here! Towards the end of the series, during some clearing up of the jungle camp, fellow celebrity Tara Palmer-Tomkinson gingerly plucked from the midden an item of clothing, held it aloft, and declaimed, magisterially, 'These are Uri's underpants. Burn them!'

George I (English king, 1660–1727). Having divorced his wife and kept her confined in a German castle for the rest of her life, George kept two mistresses. One, Ehrengard Melusine von der Schulenburg, Duchess of Kendal, was rakishly thin. The other, Charlotte Sophia von Kielmannsegg, Countess of Darlington, was enormously plump. Horace Walpole left a vivid pen-portrait of her: 'Lady Darlington, whom I saw at my mother's in my infancy, and whom I remember by being terrified at her enormous figure, was as corpulent and ample as the Duchess was long and emaciated. Two fierce black eyes, large and rolling beneath two lofty arched eyebrows, two acres of cheeks spread with crimson, an ocean of neck that overflowed and was not distinguished from the lower parts of her body, and no part restrained by stays – no wonder that a child dreaded such an ogress, and that the mob of London were highly diverted at the importation of so uncommon a seraglio!'

George III (English king, 1738–1820). George III banned the wearing of spectacles in the royal court.

George V (English king, 1865–1936). In a radio broadcast shortly after George V's death, the Archbishop of Canterbury remarked that the King had a conspicuously small head.

Gerhardie, William (English writer, 1895–1977). In St Petersburg in 1918, Gerhardie was about to be set upon by a tangle of angry Bolsheviks when one of them recognised him and pointed out to his pals that it was 'Geerhardi, Geerhardi'. Mistaking the foppish young Englishman for Keir Hardie, founder of the Labour Party and socialist saint, the revolutionaries shook Gerhardie by the hand instead of tearing him limb from limb.

Gibson, Willie (Irish, 2nd Baron Ashbourne, 1868–1942). An enthusiastic Gaelic nationalist, Gibson was rumoured to keep a tortoise in his sporran.

Gilbert, William (English physicist, 1544–1603). In his 1600 work, *On the magnet, magnetick bodies also, and on the great magnet the earth,* Gilbert asked if this whole book-writing lark was worth the trouble. 'But why should I,' he wrote, 'in so vast an Ocean of Books by which the minds of studious men are troubled and fatigued, through which very foolish productions the world and unreasoning men are intoxicated, and puffed up, rave and create literary broils, and while professing to be philosophers, physicians, mathematicians and astrologers, neglect and despise men of learning: why should I, I say, add aught further to this so-perturbed republick of letters, and expose this noble philosophy, which seems new and incredible by reason of so many things hitherto unrevealed, to be damned and torn to pieces by the maledictions of those who are either already sworn to the opinions of other men, or are foolish corruptors of good arts, learned idiots, grammatists, sophists, wranglers, and perverse little folk?'

Gillray, James (English artist, 1756/7–1815). Towards the end of his life, racked by gout, with failing eyesight, and drinking too much, the caricaturist Gillray went mad, and was confined to the upper floor of a printmaker's shop in St James' Street. He could often be seen peering out of the windows, raving. One day he defenestrated himself, and later died of the injuries caused by his fall.

Gladstone, William Ewart (English politician and Prime Minister, 1809–98). In August 1892, Gladstone's wife wrote to Queen Victoria to report that the octogenarian statesman had been attacked by a reprehensible cow. It charged at him in a field and knocked him off his feet. The cow glared at Gladstone. Gladstone glared back. Eventually he managed to get up and dart behind a tree, whereupon the cow forgot about him and wandered away. In spite of this retreat, the cow was shot. *See* Machen, Arthur

Goddard, Doris (English communicant with space people, twentieth century). The wife of space people communicant Jimmy Goddard (q.v.), Doris sometimes mistook strange extraterrestrial spacecraft swooping across the sky in curiously bird-like motion for actual birds.

Goddard, Jimmy (English communicant with space people, b. 1946). One of Goddard's earliest direct contacts with space people took place at Salisbury railway station in 1966. Suspecting that he was 'virtually living on half a brain', he was advised by communications to wear a copper cone on his head to help with his condition. Misunderstanding, and thinking they meant an Atlantean copper cone with complicated circuits, Goddard told the space people he felt unqualified to make one. They shouted back at him that a simple copper cone ought not be beyond his wit. Their impatient and irritated tone surprised him. Subsequently he asked his father to make a cone for him from a piece of scrap sheet copper, and wore it daily. He found it helped much better than the rudimentary brain scanner he had built some years earlier.

Goering, Hermann (German Nazi, 1893–1946). At the 1938 Munich Conference, Goering changed his uniform several times a day in order to impress the visiting delegates. 'He would have impressed Chamberlain far more if he had talked to him about scaup ducks', recalled Alec Douglas-Home.

Goldsmith, Oliver (English-Irish writer, 1730–74). Despite being neither a naturalist nor an historian, Goldsmith wrote an eight-volume work entitled *An History of the Earth and Animated Nature*, published posthumously. It includes the useful information that Lapland squirrels construct little rafts and, in their thousands, sail across the great lakes fanning themselves with their tails.

Goodwin, Fred (Scottish banker, b. 1958). The man who brought the Royal Bank of Scotland crashing down displayed 'a particular horror of any public use of Sellotape'. His other phobias included peanuts, carpets, false teeth, Christmas cards, violins, filing cabinets, and pink wafer biscuits. *See* Hauser, Kaspar

Gorey, Edward (American illustrator and writer, 1925–2000). The two people Gorey hated more than anyone else in the world were Henry James and Pablo Picasso. In his later years he produced amateur dramatics stage versions of his works, with 'goofy casting'. The part of the ballerina Maudie Splaytoe in *The Gilded Bat* was played by a six-foot-four black man, who was 'absolutely hilarious'.

Gosse, Edmund (English writer, 1849–1928). Gosse's birth was noted in his father Philip's diary as follows: 'Received green swallow from Jamaica. E delivered of a son.'

Gould, John M. (American outdoorsman, 1839–1930). In his 1877 book, *How To Camp Out*, Gould gave an indispensable list of things to pack for a camping trip. He prefaced it with two caveats, first that the list is by no means exhaustive, and second that one should avoid being overloaded. The following items, however, were deemed essential: Axe (in cover). Axle-grease. Bacon. Barometer (pocket). Bean-pot. Beans (in bag). Beef (dried). Beeswax. Bible. Blacking and brush. Blankets. Boxes. Bread for lunch. Brogans (oiled). Broom. Butter-dish and cover. Canned goods. Chalk. Cheese. Clothes-brush. Cod-line. Coffee and pot. Comb. Compass. Condensed milk. Cups. Currycomb. Dates. Dippers. Dishes. Dish-towels. Drawers. Dried fruits. Dutch oven. Envelopes. Figs. Firkin. Fishing-tackle. Flour (prepared). Frying-pan. Guide-book. Half-barrel. Halter. Hammer. Hard-bread. Harness (examine!). Hatchet. Haversack. Ink (portable bottle). Knives (sheath, table, pocket and butcher). Lemons. Liniment. Lunch for day or two. Maps. Matches and safe. Marline. Meal (in bag). Meal-bag. Medicines. Milk-can. Molasses. Money ('change'). Monkey-wrench. Mosquito-bar. Mustard and pot. Nails. Neat's-foot oil. Night-shirt. Oatmeal. Oil-can.

Opera-glass. Overcoat. Padlock and key. Pails. Paper. Paper collars. Pens. Pepper. Pickles. Pins. Portfolio. Postage stamps. Postal cards. Rope. Rubber blanket. Rubber coat. Rubber boots. Sail-needle. Salt. Salt fish. Salt pork. Salve. Saw. Shingles (for plates). Shirts. Shoes and strings. Slippers. Soap. Song-book. Spade. Spoons. Stove (utensils in bags). Sugar. Tea. Tents. Tent poles. Tent pins. Toothbrush. Towels. Twine. Vinegar. Watch and key.

Grainger, Percy (Australian composer, 1882–1961). Grainger wrote a pen-portrait of his mother, Rose, entitled 'Mother's Wilfulness, Recklessness, Fearlessness, Bossiness, Violence If Opposed, Tendency To Burn Food When Cooking, Vehemence'.

Green, Abdur Raheem (English Muslim convert, formerly Anthony Green, b. 1962). Ampleforth-educated Green is a former Roman-Catholic convert to Islam. He knows what lies in store for infidels and described it in a television broadcast. Hell, apparently, is a place of the most extreme pain and suffering imaginable – torments that are equally physical, mental, and spiritual. Your skin will burn, and then Allah will give you a new skin, and burn that too. When you cry out for something to drink, you will be given water, but it will be boiling water and it will burn your insides. You will also be given drink from a river of pus oozing from the wounds of your fellow sufferers in Hell. For food, you will be allowed to eat the fruits of the tree of Zakum. These fruits are so bitter, like the heads of devils, that they are barely edible, but you will force yourself to eat them, because there is nothing else to eat. In Hell you neither live nor die, you are in despair, and spend eternity arguing rancorously, surrounded by fire. As if that is not enough, 'the smallest punishment of the hellfire is that a person will wear a pair of sandals of fire, and their brain will boil'.

Greene, Graham (English writer, 1904–91). Greene lost his virginity to a much older woman. While in the middle of things, a bird flew in through an open window and flapped panic-stricken around the room, crashing into the walls.

Grimaldi, Joseph (English actor and clown, 1778–1827). Grimaldi's father came to England from Genoa to serve as Queen Charlotte's dentist. He abandoned this post to become an entertainer, and introduced the infant Joseph into his act, as a monkey. On one occasion, Grimaldi senior was swinging the 'monkey' round on a chain when the chain broke and the boy was hurled into the theatre audience, where his fall was broken by the lap of a gentle-man 'who was sitting gazing at the stage with intense interest'. Grimaldi went on to become the most success-ful clown of the age. In his leisure time he bred pigeons and collected insects. *See* Jones, Jim

Griswold, Rufus Wilmot (American editor and critic, 1815–57). Griswold was known as 'the pedagogue vam-pire' by his contemporaries. He appointed himself as Edgar Allan Poe's (q.v.) literary executor, with the sole intention of destroying Poe's reputation. In *Edgar Allan Poe After Fifty Years*, William Fearing Gill wrote: 'In view of the fact that the Griswold biography of Poe has been incontestably discredited, and proved to be merely a scaffolding of malevolent falsehoods – the outcome of malice and mendacity – the deference paid to Griswold and his baleful work in the memoir accompanying the latest publication of Poe's writings seems well-nigh incomprehensible.'

Guinefort (French saint, thirteenth century). Should you offer prayers to St Guinefort, you should bear in mind that in life he was a dog, a French greyhound to be precise. Wrongly thought to have eaten a baby, Guinefort was killed by his master, a knight, but it was then discovered that he had in fact tried to save the baby from a viper. Realising his error, the knight threw the dead dog down a well and built a shrine around it. Local people soon began worshipping Guinefort and it was said he could protect infants. A contemporary chronicler described the goings-on at the shrine: 'The local peasants hearing of the dog's noble deed and innocent death, began to visit the place and honour the dog as a martyr in quest of help for their sicknesses and other needs. They were seduced and often cheated by the Devil so that he might in this way lead men into error. Women especially, with sick or poorly children, carried them to the place, and went off a league to another nearby castle where an old woman could teach them a ritual for making offerings and invocations to the demons and lead them to the right spot. When they got there, they offered salt and certain other things, hung the child's little clothes on the bramble bushes around, fixing them on the thorns. They then put the naked baby through the opening between the trunks of two trees, the mother standing on one side and throwing her child nine times to the old woman on the other side, while invoking the demons to adjure the fauns in the wood of Rimite to take the sick and failing child which they said belonged to them (the fauns) and return to them their own child big, plump, live and healthy. Once this was done, the killer mothers took the baby and placed it naked at the foot of the tree on the straws of a cradle, lit at both ends two candles a thumbsbreadth thick with fire they had brought with them and fastened them on the trunk above. Then, while the candles were consumed, they went far enough away that they could neither hear nor see the child. In this way the burning candles burned up and killed a number of babies, as we have heard from others in the same place.' Although never sanctioned by the Catholic Church, the cult of Saint Guinefort persisted into the 1930s.

Handl, Irene (English actress, 1901–87). Irene Handl became famous for playing broad Cockneys. In fact she was the daughter of Viennese aristocrats.

Hardy, G. H. (English mathematician, 1877–1947). Hardy, together with fellow mathematician Srinivasa Ramanujan, gives his name to the Hardy-Ramanujan Number, 1729. His Indian colleague was ill in hospital and Hardy went to see him. He recalled, 'I had ridden in taxi cab number 1729 and remarked that the number seemed to me rather a dull one, and that I hoped it was not an unfavourable omen. "No," [Ramanujan] replied. "It is a very interesting number; it is the smallest number expressible as the sum of two cubes in two different ways."' *See* Willis, Bruce

Hardy, Thomas (English writer, 1840–1928) *See* Cowley, Sir John Guise *and* Newbolt, Henry

Harmsworth, Alfred, Lord Northcliffe (English newspaper magnate, 1865–1922). One day at a seaside resort, Northcliffe wantonly struck down a seagull with his stick and beat it to death on the sand.

Harvey, Gabriel (English writer, *c.* 1552–1631). Harvey was the great enemy of Thomas Nashe, who attacked him in *Strange Newes, of the Intercepting Certaine Letters*, thus: 'There is a Doctor and his Fart that haue kept a foule stinking stirre in Paules Churchyard ; I crie him mercy, I slaundered him, he is scarce a Doctor till he hath done his Acts ; this dodipoule, this didopper, this professed poetical braggart hath raild vpon me, without wit or art, in certaine foure penniworth of Letters and three farthing-worth of Sonnets ; nor do I mean to present him and *Shakerley* to the Queens foole-taker for coatch-horses: for two that draw more equallie in one Oratoriall yoke of vaine-glorie, there is not vnder heauen. . . why thou arrant butter whore, thou cotqueane & scrattop of scoldes, wilt thou neuer leaue afflicting a dead Carcasse, continually read the rethorick lecture of Ramme Allie? a wispe, a wispe, rippe, rippe, you kitchin-stuffe wrangler!'

Hauser, Kaspar (German enigma, feral child, 1812–33). The doctor who cared for Kaspar Hauser was befuddled by the variety of things that caused him distress. He was unhinged by thunderstorms, the full moon, brandy, loud noises, quiet noises, squeezed cheese, bright daylight, beer, cats, spiders, snakes, flowers, grape juice, beards, the colour black and comedy. *See* Lutyens, Sir Edwin

Hawker, Stephen (English clergyman, 1803–75). Hawker was for many years the vicar of Morwenstow in Cornwall. He talked to birds, dressed up as a mermaid, excommunicated his cat, had a pet pig, and spent much of his time smoking opium in a clifftop hut made from driftwood. When his wife died he became very depressed and convinced himself he could eat nothing but clotted cream.

As a result of this diet, he grew increasingly bilious, and even more depressed.

Hawtrey, Charles (English actor, 1914–88). When his house in the Kentish port of Deal caught fire in 1984, Hawtrey went downstairs to raise the alarm and then deliberately went up to the top storey so he would have to be carried down a ladder by one of the big burly firemen to whom he was so attracted. As he was naked, the fireman gave him his helmet to cover his modesty. Hawtrey put the helmet on his head as he did not want to be seen without his wig. He was barred from most of the pubs in Deal as a cantankerous drunk.

Haydn, Joseph (Austrian composer, 1732–1809). Haydn's wife Anna was a religious maniac who, according to the composer's friend Carpani, 'wanted the house always full of priests'. Not only did the constant guests eat Haydn out of house and home, but they demanded – through Anna – a stream of musical compositions. Carpani relates that 'Mrs. Anna [always] had a new request; to-day a responsory, to-morrow a motet, the day after a mass, then hymns, then psalms, then antiphons; and all gratis. If her husband declined to write them, there appeared on the scene the great confederates of capricious women; the effects of hysteria, spleen, spasms; then shrieks, then criminations, weepings, quarrels, and bad humour unceasing. Haydn ended with having to appease the woman, to lose his point, and pay the doctor and the druggist to boot. He had always drouth in his purse and despair in his mind. It is a true miracle that a genius in such a contrast could create the wonderful works that all the world knows.'

Heiney, Paul (English journalist and broadcaster, b. 1949). Heiney was once told by an old man of the hills that sheep have only one ambition in life, and that is to die.

Heliogabalus (Roman Emperor, *c.* 203–22). According to Alexandre Dumas, in the preface to his *Grand Dictionnaire de Cuisine*, 'Heliogabalus made elaborate preparations for his own death, expecting that it would come in the midst of some uprising. He had a courtyard in his palace paved with porphyry so that he might throw himself down on it from a high place. He had a steel dagger fitted with a diamond-studded, carved gold hilt, to stab himself. He had especially spun a rope of gold and silk, to strangle himself. Surprised in the latrine by his assassins, he choked himself to death on the sponge that, to use Montaigne's expression, "the Romans used to wipe their behinds".'

Hemmerde, Edward (English barrister and politician, 1871–1948). Hemmerde was variously described as a profligate, a wastrel, a stormy petrel, a soured man, a good-time Charlie, an 'irrepressible, loud-mouthed, honourable and outspoken braggart', and 'a man who was much maligned and misunderstood'. When he was overexcited – which was most of the time – his voice rose to an ear-splitting high-pitched screech.

Henman, Tim (English tennis player, b. 1974). Henman has pointed out that when any group of people see a swan, one among their number will always remark that these graceful yet savage birds are capable of breaking a person's arm. He goes on to note the curious fact that, contrarily, nobody has ever met anybody who has had their arm broken by a swan. *See* Hensley, Anthony

Henry VII (British king, 1457–1509). Like most medieval kings, Henry collected holy relics. His most treasured possession was an entire leg said to belong to Saint George. He once ordered that all the mastiffs in England be hanged, on the basis that they would attack a lion, the lion being symbolic of the king. He is the only adult monarch between Edward I and Henry VIII about whom not one Elizabethan or Jacobean dramatist wrote a play.

Hensley, Anthony (American swan care and maintenance operative, 1974/75–2012). After paddling his kayak too close to a swan in Des Plaines, Illinois, Hensley was attacked and killed by one or more of the graceful yet savage birds. *See* Hericks, Hermann-Josef

Heppenstall, Rayner (English writer, 1911–81). His father encouraged Heppenstall to learn Esperanto, but he soon threw in the towel. 'I could no longer take it seriously,' he wrote, 'when I found the word for "bird" was "birdo".'

Hericks, Hermann-Josef (German hotelier, twenty-first century). Not all hoteliers need tractors, but Hericks bought one in 2008. A local swan promptly fell in love with it, following it everywhere. Animal behaviourist Daniela Fiutak concluded that the swan 'presumably had contact with machines during puberty. He sees the tractor as a sexual partner.' *See* Hugh of Lincoln

Herkomer, Hubert von (German-English painter, 1849–1914). The costumes, ceremonies and paraphernalia of ancient Welsh druidry, as celebrated in the Eisteddfod, were inadvertently invented by Herkomer in a series of 'history' paintings done at his studio in Bushey, Hertfordshire.

Heubeck, Werner Wolfgang (German bus manager, 1923–2009). As the manager of Belfast municipal bus services at the height of the Troubles, Heubeck was known for his hands-on approach. He personally removed hundreds of suspect devices planted on buses while dressed in his raincoat and trilby. When he retired, he asked for his leaving present to be a large quantity of wood. He then spent his time making hand-carved artefacts, which he donated to churches throughout the province. He later moved to Shetland, where he busied himself making fruitcakes and cushions for charity shops.

Heurn, Willem Cornelis van (Dutch naturalist, 1887–1972). Van Heurn published more than 100 papers on extremely specific matters in natural history that nobody had ever thought to address before. These included *Do tits lay eggs together as the result of a housing shortage?; Poaching in the service of ornithology; A gecko with a forked tail; Cannibalism in frogs; Mortality of chicken broods during a thunderstorm; Wrinkled eggs; Extra premolars in the lower jaw of the mole; Our cat washes herself; Some comments on the bats of Buitenzorg; The rat question; Shark and ray leather; The safety instinct in chickens;* and *An observation of a cuckoo which, without evidence, would have been falsely interpreted.*

Hewson, Paul (Irish businessman, b. 1960). Hewson prefers to be known as 'Bono', which is a popular brand of dog biscuit.

Hibberd, Shirley (English horticulturist, 1825–90). Hibberd was a prolific author of books on gardening and other topics. Among his publications were *Rustic Adorn-ments For Homes Of Taste* (1856); *The Seaweed Collector: A Handy Guide To The Marine Botanist Suggesting What To Look For, And Where To Go In The Study Of The British Algae And The British Sponges* (1872); *Clever Dogs, Horses, Etc* (1868); and *Water-Cresses Without Sewage* (1878).

Hitchcock, Alfred (English film director, 1899–1980). The Master of Suspense was terrified of eggs. In a 1963 interview, he said: 'I'm frightened of eggs, worse than frightened, they revolt me. That white round thing without any holes. . . have you ever seen anything more revolting than an egg yolk breaking and spilling its yellow liquid? Blood is jolly, red. But egg yolk is yellow, revolting. I've never tasted it.' *See* Obama, Barack

Hitchens, Peter (English writer, b. 1951). On the final day of 2010, Hitchens wrote, magnificently, 'I am actively hostile to the "New Year", a celebration of nothing in particular.'

Hohman, John George (German-American writer, six-teenth century). Hohman devised a method of angling guaranteed to catch fish. Dangle a net in a river or lake, and fish will be sure to collect there if you have first placed in the net rose seed, mustard seed, and the foot of a weasel.

Holliday, Robert Cortes (American writer, 1880–1947).

Among the things revealed by Holliday in his *Walking-Stick Papers* was the fact that, on the Isle of Wight in the 1890s, an official bye-law stated: 'As to Bears: No bear shall be taken along or allowed to be upon any highway, unless such bear shall be securely confined in a vehicle closed so as to completely hide such bear from view.'

Holmes, Sherlock (Fictional amateur sleuth). Dr John Watson's chronicle of the career of Sherlock Holmes is far from exhaustive. In the course of his narratives, he makes passing mention of a number of cases of which no further details are forthcoming, to wit, Von Bischoff of Frankfurt, Mason of Bradford, the notorious Muller, Lefevre and Leturier of Montpellier, Samson of New Orleans, Van Jansen of Utrecht, the Ratcliff Highway murders, Dolsky of Odessa, the wills in Riga in 1857 and St Louis in 1871, Mrs Cecil Forrester's domestic complication, the woman who poisoned three children for their insurance money, similar cases in India and Senegambia, the Bishopsgate jewels, the Trepoff murder, the Atkinson brothers at Trincomalee, the mission for the Dutch royal family, the Darlington substitution scandal, the business at Arnsworth castle, the Dundas separation case, that intricate matter in Marseilles, the disappearance of Mr Etheredge, the similar cases in Andover and The Hague, the adventure of the Paradol Chamber, the Amateur Mendicant Society, the loss of the barque *Sophie Anderson*, the Grice Patersons on Uffa, the Camberwell poisoning, the Tankerville Club scandal, two murders, the throwing of vitriol, suicide and a number of robberies associated with the Blue Carbuncle, Mrs Farintosh and the opal tiara, the madness of Colonel Warburton, the Grosvenor Square furniture van, the King of Scandinavia and similar cases in Aberdeen and Munich, the affair of the bogus laundry, the Tarleton murders, Vamberry the wine merchant, the old Russian woman, the singular affair of the aluminium crutch, the club-footed Ricoletti and his abominable wife, Baron Maupertuis and the Netherland-Sumatra Company, the Worthingdon bank robbery, Adams and the Manor House, the tired captain, the French Government case in Nîmes and Narbonne, the Scandinavian royal family, the Vatican cameos, Wilson of the district messenger office, the Grodno blackmail and others, Little Russia, the Anderson murders in North Carolina, the Colonel Upwood card scandal at the Nonpareil Club, Madame Montpensier's murder charge against her daughter, the Molesey Mystery, Morgan the poisoner, Merridew of abominable memory, Matthews who knocked out Holmes's left canine in the waiting room at Charing Cross, the murder of Mrs Stewart in Lauder, the papers of ex-President Murillo, the Dutch steamship *Friesland*, Bert Stevens the murderer, the persecution of tobacco millionaire John Vincent Harden, Archie Stamford the forger, the Ferrers documents, the Abergavenny murder, the death of Cardinal Tosca, Wilson the canary trainer, the dreadful business of the Abernetty family, the Conk-Singleton forgery, Crosby the banker and the red leech, the contents of the Addleton barrow, the Smith-Mortimer succession case, Huret the Boulevard Assassin, Arthur H. Staunton the forger and Henry Staunton, the Randall burglars of Lewisham, the Margate woman, Colonel Carruthers, Brooks, Woodhouse, Fairdale Hobbs, the Long Island cave mystery, Abrahams in mortal terror, Rotherhithe, old Baron Dowson, the disappearances of James Phillimore and of the cutter *Alicia*, the madness of Isadora Persano, the ship *Matilda Briggs* and the giant rat of Sumatra, the forger Victor Lynch, Vittoria the circus belle, Vanderbilt and the Yeggman, Vigor the Hammersmith Wonder, Sir George Lewis and the Hammerford Will, Wainwright, the Duke of Greyminster and Abbey School, the Sultan of Turkey's commission, two Coptic patriarchs, the St Pancras picture-frame maker, and a coiner, not to forget the case of the politician, the lighthouse and the trained cormorant.

Home, Daniel Dunglas (Scottish medium, 1833–86). Home was the most famous of all nineteenth-century spiritualist mediums, counting among his devotees Napoleon III and the Empress Eugénie, William Makepeace Thackeray, John Ruskin, Sir Edward Bulwer-Lytton, Harriet Beecher Stowe, and a panoply of crowned heads and aristocrats. When he married his first wife, his best man was Alexandre Dumas, and his son Gregory's godfather was Tsar Alexander II. Gregory's birth was attended by signs and portents, spirit-lights, and the singing of invisible birds. One of Home's greatest admirers was Elizabeth Barrett Browning; his most implacable enemy was Robert Browning, who cast him as Mr. Sludge The Medium in his poem of that name.

Hope, Terence (English brain surgeon, b. 1946). Hope was a consultant neurologist who was suspended from duty at his hospital after allegedly taking an extra helping of soup in the canteen without paying. Hope protested that he had merely been taking some extra croutons. He was later reinstated after the matter was raised in the House of Lords.

Hopkins, Gerard Manley (English Jesuit and poet,

1844–89). On 27 April 1871, Hopkins noted in his journal that he mesmerised a duck. He did not say why.

Horn, Henry J. (American medium, nineteenth century). Horn was able to communicate with the spirits of many illustrious dead, and in 1871 published *Strange Visitors, A Series Of Original Papers, Embracing Philosophy, Science, Government, Religion, Poetry, Art, Fiction, Satire, Humor, Narrative, And Prophecy, By The Spirits Of Irving, Willis, Thackeray, Bronte, Richter, Byron, Humboldt, Hawthorne, Wesley, Browning, And Others Now Dwelling In The Spirit World, Dictated Through A Clairvoyant, While In An Abnormal Or Trance State.*

Horniman, John (English tea merchant and philanthropist, 1803–93). Horniman invented the tea bag. His son John Frederick Horniman was an avid collector of antiquities and curios from around the world, amassing so many items in his south London house that his wife insisted either the collection had to go or she would. He bought a nearby property, moved his family into it, and gave the original house over to the collection, still thriving as the Horniman Museum.

Howard, Trevor (English actor, 1913–88). Howard earned the respect of his peers by recounting his brave military past, parachuting into Nazi-occupied Norway and taking part in the Allied invasion of Sicily. After his death, Public Record Office files revealed that he had been invalided out of the army on account of mental instability and a 'psychopathic personality'.

Howerd, Frankie (English comedian, 1917–92). Howerd's childhood ambition was to become a saint. When instead he turned to the theatre he appeared under the stage names Ronnie Ordex and Frankie Howerd The Borderline Case. At a RADA audition he performed the soliloquy from *Hamlet* while clutching his packed lunch. The bag split and covered his audience with bread and cheese.

Hubbard, L. Ron (American mountebank, 1911–86). The Ur-text of Scientology is Hubbard's book *Excalibur*, which contains the secrets of the universe. His best-selling *Dianetics* was based on a single chapter of the earlier work. Written in a six-day frenzy after Hubbard was apparently clinically dead for eight minutes following a dental extraction, *Excalibur* was later advertised thus: 'Mr Hubbard wrote this work in 1938. When four of the first fifteen people who read it went insane, Mr Hubbard withdrew it and placed it in a vault where it remained until now. Copies to selected readers only and then on signature. Released only on sworn statement not to permit other readers to read it. Contains data not to be released during Mr Hubbard's stay on earth . . . Facsimile of original, individually typed for manuscript buyer. Gold bound and locked. Signed by author. Very limited. Per copy $1,500.00.'

Hübner, Julius (German artist, 1806–82). In 1851, *Harper's New Monthly Magazine* reported: 'In the album presented to the King of Bavaria by the artists of Münich, is an admirable composition by Hübner. It is an expression of the feelings of a large portion of Upper Germany. It represents a female prostrate upon the ground, with the arms crossed, the face entirely hidden, in an attitude of the deepest despair. The long hair floats over the arms, and trails along the ground. The whole figure is a mixture of majesty and utter abandonment. The simple title of the piece is – *Germania, 1850.*'

Huddesford, George (English poet, 1749–1809). Huddesford's works included the poem *The scum uppermost when the Middlesex porridge-pot boils over: an heroic election ballad with explanatory notes: accompanied with an admonitory nod to a blind horse* (1802). He also wrote *Bubble And Squeak: A Gallimaufry of British Beef with the Chopped Cabbage of Gallic Philosophy* (1799).

Hudson, Henry (English explorer, *c.* 1565–1611). Hudson was said to possess 'the combinations rare enough of talent, invincible courage, patience and fortitude under suffering, daring, enterprise tempered by prudence, promptness and decision, united with calm reflection, sagacity, fertility of invention, strong common-sense, combined with enthusiasm and vivid imagination, the power of commanding other minds, joined to gentleness of manner and ready sympathy'. Unfortunately, however, he was an incompetent navigator who often had no idea where he was going. On one of his first voyages he discovered a mermaid (who 'looked earnestly upon the men until the sea overturned her') and two fragments of the true cross which had somehow found their way to Greenland.

Hugh of Lincoln (English saint, 1135/40–1200). Hugh is the patron saint of swans. He developed a deep and lasting friendship with a white swan from the Lincolnshire town of Stowe. The swan followed him everywhere he went, guarded him while he slept, and attacked anyone who came near him. *See* Pavlova, Anna

Hughes, Howard (American tycoon, 1905–76). During the 1930s, Hughes's friends noted that he had become obsessed with the size of peas. He used a specially-designed fork to arrange the peas on his plate from smallest to largest. *See* Stendahl

Hughes, Ted (English poet, 1930–98). In the 1960s, in collaboration with the theatre director Peter Brook, Hughes devised a new language called Orghast. Earthy and primal, Orghast would be able to express things ordinary namby-pamby languages could not. It eventually had a vocabulary of about two thousand words, but of these only fifty counted as 'Real Orghast'. A standard phrase such as 'darkness opens its womb' translates into Orghast as BULLORGA OMBOLOM FROR.

Hunt, William Leonard (Canadian funambulist, 1838–1929). As 'The Great Farini', Hunt crossed the Niagara Falls on a tightrope in 1860. His other feats included walking a high wire while completely covered by a sack. After his retirement from the tightrope, he was for a time manager of the Royal Aquarium and Summer and Winter Garden in London. There he put on acts including the human cannonball, Pongo the Gorilla, manatee 'mermaids', and the Beckwith family, who, while submerged in one of the aquarium tanks, undressed, smoked, and ate two sponge cakes.

Huston, Anjelica (American actress, b. 1951). Anjelica Huston's first screen role was in *A Walk With Love And Death* (1969), directed by her father John Huston. The critic John Simon wrote: 'There is a perfectly blank, supremely inept performance by Huston's daughter

Anjelica, who has the face of an exhausted gnu, the voice of an unstrung tennis racket, and a figure of no discernible shape.' This is the only review of her work that Huston quotes in her autobiography.

Ilg, Alfred (Swiss engineer, 1854–1916). Ilg designed the cupola of the Observatory in Berne, Switzerland and the waterworks of both Berne and Addis Ababa. He created the Ethiopian postal system, supervised the electrification of the royal palace in Addis Ababa, made a pair of shoes and a rifle for Haile Selassie's uncle, sported Ruritanian tinpot attire, and was a close friend of Arthur Rimbaud.

Ironside, Robin (English artist, 1912–65). Ironside was a chain-smoking, mescaline-taking visionary. His paintings were given titles such as *Street Entertainer Playing Threatening Music To A Cinema Queue*; *A Picture To Prove That The Greeks Only Painted With Three Colours*; *Wounded Man In Bed-sitting Room*; *Crowd Awaiting A Portent*; *Famous Statues Visiting A Museum Of People*; and *Patients Suffering From Waxy Insensibility*. He designed a four-foot obelisk in Sevenhampton churchyard to commemorate Ian Fleming.

Ives, Charles (American composer, 1874–1954). An insurance executive who composed in his spare time, Ives heard very few public performances of his work. One of his rare opportunities was a concert given in New York on 10 January 1931, where his *Three Places In New England* was programmed alongside works by Henry Cowell and Carl

Ruggles. Ives nearly ruined the concert, however, when, hearing a man in the row behind him hissing, he leapt to his feet and shouted, 'You goddam sissy! When you hear strong masculine music like this, get up and use your ears like a man!'

Jacobs, Michael (English art historian and travel writer, 1952–2014). Jacobs was a *bon viveur* with a taste for adventure. This was a reaction against his childhood, where spontaneity and entertainment were frowned upon. On Thursdays it was forbidden to speak except in Latin.

James I (English king, also James VI of Scotland, 1566–1625). James was one of the first anti-smoking campaigners. In his *A Counterblast To Tobacco* (1604) he called it 'a custome loathsome to the eye, hateful to the nose, harmfull to the braine, dangerous to the lungs, and in the blacke stinking fume thereof neerest resembling the horrible Stigian smoake of the pit that is bottomlesse.'

James II (English king, 1633–1701). In the *Mémoires du Comte de Gramont*, Antoine Hamilton described James II's (unsuccessful) wooing of Lady Elizabeth Hamilton: 'He entertained her with what he had in his head; telling her miracles of the cunning of foxes and the mettle of horses; giving her accounts of broken legs and arms, dislocated shoulders, and other curious and entertaining adventures; after which his eyes told her the rest.'

Jameson, Anna Brownell (Irish writer, 1794–1860). The young Anna Jameson travelled through Italy as a governess. She was not wholly impressed. 'We have visited the pretty English burial-ground, and the tomb of Smollet, which in the true English style is cut and scratched all over with the names of fools, who think thus to link their own insignificance to his immortality. We have also seen whatever else is to be seen, and what all travellers describe: to-morrow we leave Leghorn – for myself without regret: it is a place with which I have no sympathies, and the hot, languid, damp atmosphere, which depresses the spirits and relaxes the nerves, has made me suffer ever since we arrived.'

Jansson, Tove (Finnish writer and illustrator, 1914–2001). When staying at her Finnish island retreat, it was Tove Jansson's practice to get out of bed at four o'clock in the morning and stand stock-still, pretending to be a tree, while a squirrel ran up and down her frozen limbs.

Jantjie, Thamsanqa (South African sign language interpreter, twenty-first century). Jantjie was employed as the sign language interpreter at the memorial service for Nelson Mandela on 10 December 2013. Rather than using any recognisable signing system, however, Jantjie's 'interpretation' of speeches by luminaries such as Presidents Barack Obama and Jacob Zuma consisted of random hand gestures which translated as gibberish. Apologising after the event, Jantjie explained that 'What happened that day . . . I see angels come to the stadium. I start realising that the problem is here. Sometimes I react violent on that place. Sometimes I will see things that chase me. I was in a very difficult position. And remember, those people, the president and everyone, they were armed. There was armed police around me. If

100

I start panicking I'll start being a problem. I have to deal with this in a manner so that I mustn't embarrass my country.' Asked how often he had become violent in the past, he replied 'a lot'.

Jennings, Hargrave (English occultist, 1817–90). In his book *Curious Things Of The Outside World: Last Fire* (1861), Jennings gave a helpful historical summary of swoons, shudders, convulsions and dread: 'Amatus Lusitanus relates the case of a monk who fainted when he beheld a rose, and never quitted his cell while that flower was blooming. Orfila (a less questionable authority) gives the account of the painter Vincent, who was seized with violent vertigo, and swooned, when there were roses in the room. Voltaire gives the history of an officer who was thrown into convulsions and lost his senses by having pinks in his chamber. Orfila also relates the instance of a lady, of forty-six years of age, of a hale constitution, who could never be present when a decoction of linseed was preparing, being troubled in the course of a few minutes with a general swelling of the face, followed by fainting and a loss of the intellectual faculties, which symptoms continued for four-and-twenty hours. Montaigne remarks on this subject, that there were men who dreaded an apple more than a cannon-ball. Zimmerman tells us of a lady who could not endure the feeling of silk and satin, and shuddered when she touched the velvety skin of a peach; other ladies cannot bear the feel of fur. Boyle records the case of a man who experienced a natural abhorrence of honey; a young man invariably fainted when a servant swept his room. Hippocrates mentions one Nicanor, who swooned whenever he heard a flute; and Shakespeare has alluded to the strange effect of the bagpipe. Boyle fell into a syncope when he heard the splashing of water; Scaliger turned pale on the sight of water-cresses; Erasmus experienced febrile symptoms when smelling fish; the Duke d'Epernon swooned on beholding a leveret, although a hare did not produce the same effect; Tycho Brahe fainted at the sight of a fox, Henry III of France at that of a cat, and Marshal D'Albret at a pig. The horror that whole families entertain of cheese is well known.'

Jeronima Of The Assumption (Spanish nun, 1555–1630). In her mid-sixties, Jeronima sailed from Spain to establish the first convent in the Philippines. The Venerable Mother was renowned for her particularly austere programme of penitence. She was given to re-enacting the crucifixion by attaching herself to a cross and hanging upside down for up to three hours at a time. Her portrait was painted by Velázquez.

Johnson, Samuel (English writer, 1709–84). Johnson collected the peel of Seville oranges. Having squeezed its juice into his drink at the club, he would pop an orange into his pocket, take it home, carefully scrape the peel, cut it up and lay the pieces out on his table to dry. Questioned by Boswell as to what use he put the peel, Johnson refused to explain his conduct, with characteristic force.

Jones, Jim (American cult leader, 1931–78). Jones was the leader of the People's Temple, the cult he persuaded into mass suicide in Jonestown, Guyana in 1978. In his early days, to fund his cult-building activities, he worked as a door-to-door monkey salesman. *See* Lauri, Charles

102

Jonsdottir, Ragnhildur (Icelandic seer, twenty-first century). Jonsdottir led a campaign in 2013 to halt road-building works on the Álftanes peninsula in Iceland, claiming that the habitat of elves would be endangered. Explaining that she was in telepathic communication with the elves, she said the roadworks would be 'a terrible loss and damaging both for the elf world and for us humans'. In a survey carried out in 2007, 62 per cent of Icelanders said elves probably existed.

Joseph of Cupertino (Patron saint of pilots, astronauts, and airline passengers, 1603–63). Saint Joseph of Cupertino was nicknamed 'Open Mouth' because he wandered around in a daze with his mouth hanging open. When working in the refectory at a monastery he continually broke the crockery through his clumsiness. He often went into ecstatic trances and hovered several inches above the ground. Bishop Bonaventure Claver said that he was '*idiota*'.

Joyce, James (Irish novelist, 1882–1941). Joyce insisted on pronouncing the title of his 1922 masterpiece as *Oo-liss-iss*. Not all the early reviews were kind. *The Sphere* said *Ulysses* was 'The maddest, muddiest, most loathsome book issued in our own or any other time. . . inartistic, incoherent, unquotably nasty . . . a book that one would have thought could only emanate from a criminal lunatic asylum', while *Teachers' World* called it 'An immense mass of clotted nonsense'.

Jung, Carl Gustav (Swiss psychiatrist, 1875–1961). Jung was described by Rayner Heppenstall (q.v.) as 'perhaps the most pernicious brain-softener of our time'.

Kafka, Franz (Bohemian writer, 1883–1924). Kafka was an enthusiastic devotee of Fletcherism, the practice devised by Horace Fletcher (q.v.) of chewing each mouthful of food hundreds and hundreds of times. So disgusting were Kafka's table manners that his father used to hide behind the newspaper at dinner time to avoid having to watch his son eat.

Kaye, Danny (American entertainer, 1913–87). Kaye was a polymath. In addition to his all-singing, all-dancing stage and screen career, he was an expert chef – specialising in Chinese cooking – a skilled pilot and an honorary member of the American College of Surgeons and the American Academy of Paediatrics. He occasionally assisted top surgeons in conducting heart operations.

Keeler, Harry Stephen (American writer, 1890–1967). Keeler was a prolific writer of pulp fiction in the form of enormously lengthy, dialogue-heavy novels in which not much actually happens. In *The Man With the Magic Eardrums* (1939), for example, over hundreds of pages, a bookie and a safecracker run into each other in a house in Minneapolis and spend the night talking. There are two phone calls, and another character comes into the house and talks for a while. The direct action of *The Portrait of Jirjohn Cobb* (1940) consists of four characters, two of whom sport outrageous accents, sitting on an island in the middle of a river, talking and listening to a radio, again for hundreds of pages. Keeler was also fond of peculiarly baroque prose. *The Bottle With the Green Wax Seal* (1942) includes chapters entitled 'The Chromatic Whimsicalness of Avunculi Samuelis; Synthetic Mexican' and 'The Micro-Axially Condensed Typewriter'.

Kennedy, John Fitzgerald (American politician and POTUS, 1917–63). On a private pier in Newport, Rhode Island in September 1963, Kennedy enacted a macabre death-by-assassination fantasy. He lay seemingly lifeless, splattered with tomato juice or ketchup, while his wife Jackie and a friend stepped gingerly over him. *See* Leach, Virginia

Kennedy, Robert Francis (American politician, 1925–68). Kennedy's household pets included three dogs, plus ponies, horses, geese, a burro, a sea lion, Hungarian pigeons, twenty goldfish, rabbits, turtles and a salamander.

Killick-Kendrick, Robert (English scientist, 1929–2011). Killick-Kendrick was a research scientist, and his wife was an expert in sand flies. His real interest, however, was in bells attached to animals. He devoted much of his leisure time to studying bells worn by, *inter alia*, cows, hunting dogs, and Indian elephants. His scholarly monograph on the subject, illustrated with his own photographs, remained incomplete and unpublished at his death.

Kilvert, Francis (English clergyman and diarist, 1840–79). Kilvert thought that one of the most hateful experiences in life was to have objects pointed out to one with a stick.

Kim Jong-il (North Korean Supreme Leader, 1941–2011). One of Kim Jong-il's last official duties before he died was a visit to the newly renovated Tudan duck farm, where he enjoyed a performance given by members of the Art Squad of the Pyongyang Poultry Guidance Bureau in the newly built House of Culture at the farm.

King, George (English communicant with space people, 1919–97). King was the founder of the Aetherian Society, dedicated to improving communication with beings from outer space. He received regular messages from a Martian from Mars Sector 6. Thus he was able to advise members of the Society never to sit with their backs to the engine while on train journeys. In 1956 he forecast great hurricanes, while adding that it was likely to be an excellent season for wool.

Kipling, Rudyard (English writer, 1865–1936). Kipling was named after his parents' favourite reservoir, Lake Rudyard in Staffordshire, once known as 'the Mecca of northern match angling'. The Kiplings met and courted there, and it was rumoured to be where their son was conceived.

Kirchner, Ernst Ludwig (German artist, 1880–1938). While living in Berlin and founding Die Brücke expressionist art group as a young man, Kirchner lived a life of debauchery. He became addicted to morphine, and somehow managed to paint while drinking an entire litre of absinthe daily.

Knox, Ronald (English writer and priest, 1888–1957). One night when he was four years old, Knox was found wide awake by his nanny. She asked him what he was thinking about and he replied: 'The past.'

Kokoschka, Oskar (Austrian artist, 1886–1980). When Kokoschka and Alma Mahler visited the house they planned to move into together, they found in the bathroom an aquarium tank filled with toads. The 'hideous creatures swirling round in clusters' had been left there by one of Alma's many other admirers, a zoologist who had committed suicide a few days earlier. 'So this was his bequest to us,' wrote Kokoschka, who promptly emptied the tank of 'fat-bellied batrachians' into the swampy field surrounding the house.

Laing, Alexander Gordon (Scottish explorer, 1793–1826). While struggling through Africa on his way to Timbuctoo, Laing enumerated his wounds: two dozen sabre cuts to his head, neck, hands, arms and legs, multiple fractures, including his jaw, a split ear, a grazed windpipe, and several broken fingers. He had also been shot with a musket ball that entered through the hip and went out through his back. In addition he had caught the Plague and had most of his possessions stolen. 'I am nevertheless doing well,' he wrote, 'and hope yet to return to England with much important geographical information.' He was murdered a few days after leaving Timbuctoo.

Lamarr, Hedy (Austrian screen goddess and inventor, 1914–2000). During World War Two, together with the composer George Antheil, Hedy Lamarr patented a technique of frequency-hopping spread-spectrum radio interference designed to avert the jamming of torpedo signals. Although the technology was not adopted at the time, the US Navy made use of it from the 1960s onwards, particularly in the blockade of Cuba. It is the basis for many of today's communications developments such as Bluetooth and WiFi. Lamarr was belatedly honoured for her ground-breaking work by the Electronic Frontier Foundation in 1997.

Lambert, Richard S. (English writer, 1894–1981). Lambert was the founding editor of the BBC magazine *The Listener.* He left the post in 1939 after he was accused of being unfit for the job due to his belief in Gef the Talking Mongoose. Gef was briefly famous in the years leading up to the Second World War. He lived with – but was only once seen – by a family on the Isle of Man, to whom he announced that he had been born in New Delhi in 1834 and was, in his own reported words, 'an extra extra clever mongoose'. Gef explained that he kept out of sight because 'if you saw me you'd faint, you'd be petrified, mummified, turned into stone or a pillar of salt'. The family fed him with biscuits, chocolates and bananas, served up on a saucer suspended from the ceiling, and in return Gef helped with the housework and spied on the neighbours. Lambert co-wrote a book about Gef with the indefatigable ghost-hunter Harry Price (q.v.).

Landor, Walter Savage (English poet, 1775–1864). Landor was renowned for his irascible temperament and rambunctiousness, and argued his way across Europe. When living in the Medici Palace in Florence, he threw a cook out of the kitchen window into a flowerbed, then slapped his forehead and cried: 'My God! I forgot about the violets!'

Laszlo, Laszlo (Hungarian mountebank, 1898–1936). After a varied career involving spells as a soldier, burglar, armed robber, convict, actor, variety artist, film extra, painter, and electrotechnician, and at least two staged suicide attempts, Laszlo Laszlo became a celebrated occultist. His speciality was the production of ectoplasm, which he described as follows: 'At first I used gauze which

I soaked in water and then immersed in oil for several days. Later I ran out of oil and started to use goose-fat instead . . . I used to take the piece of gauze or cotton-wool from my accustomed hiding-place and put it in my mouth. Then the curtain was drawn apart and they could all see the "mysterious ectoplasm" hanging from my lips. No one ever dared touch it because Schrenck-Notzing had warned about this in his book, saying that it might cause the death of the medium. In any case, I accompanied it with such horrible noises that the sitters all shook in terror . . . After each séance I hid the greasy cotton-wool in my pocket and then threw it into the river on my way home.'

Lauri, Charles (English music hall artiste, 1860–1903). Lauri was a star of Drury Lane pantomime and the music halls, the 'Garrick of animal mimics', an impersonator who imitated dogs, cats, monkeys, parrots, goats, opposum, alligators, frogs, and wolves. His inspiration, as a child, was a performing monkey named Pongo. A frequent visitor to London Zoo, he spent hours observing animals in preparation for his performances. For an appearance in *Babes In The Wood*, he borrowed a poodle so he could study it. A subsequent newspaper report described him as 'the most agile performing poodle ever seen'. *See* West, Mae

Lawrence, D. H. (English writer, 1885–1930). According to Hugh Kingsmill, Lawrence was 'not a conscious charlatan, but he had an instinct for exploiting the wide areas of imbecility in the English upper classes'.

Leach, Virginia (American mystery woman, twentieth century). Of the countless mysteries surrounding the assassination of John F. Kennedy, one that has been over-looked is the identity of Virginia Leach. At the burial of Lee Harvey Oswald on 25 November 1963 at Rose Hill Cemetery in Fort Worth, two floral tributes were left at the graveside, a blanket of white carnations and a spray of red carnations, both from the mysterious Virginia Leach. *See* Oswald, Lee Harvey

Leakey, Bob (English potholer and caver, 1914–2013). Leakey was known as 'the Edmund Hillary of Potholing'. In his retirement he launched many campaigns, including one called 'Against Moneytheistic Amentia, Psychosis, & Censorship'. In 2010 he became the oldest-ever candidate at a general election when he stood in the Craven constituency for his own Virtue Currency & Cognitive Appraisal party. He polled 190 votes.

Lear, Edward (English writer and artist, 1812–88). In 1870 Lear settled in San Remo and built a luxurious residence known as Villa Emily. Some years later, when the construction of a vast hotel ruined his solitude and his sea view, he acquired a new plot of land and had a second villa built. This was the Villa Tennyson, where Lear lived for the rest of his life. He ensured that the floorplan was identical to that of the Villa Emily, so that his senile cat, Foss, could find its way around without getting lost.

Lee, Laurie (English writer, 1914–97). Lee won a school writing competition with an essay on the dabchick, a bird he thought he had invented. For the Festival of Britain in 1951 he was appointed as Caption Writer-in-Chief and Curator of Eccentricities. In old age, living back in Slad in Gloucestershire (the setting for *Cider With Rosie*) he regularly bumped into literary tourists hoping to visit his grave.

Leigh-Pemberton, Sir Robin (English banker, 1927–2013). When he was Governor in the 1980s, Leigh-Pemberton installed beehives on the roof of the Bank of England. One day when he was abroad he received a frantic telephone call from a Bank official telling him that the bees had swarmed into the offices below and were causing chaos. Asked for his advice, Leigh-Pemberton said 'Put them in a box' – and hung up the phone.

Lennon, John (English Beatle and husband of Yoko Ono, 1940–80). According to Bernard Levin (q.v.), 'there is nothing wrong with John Lennon that could not be cured by standing him upside down and shaking him gently until whatever is inside his head falls out'.

Leopold II (Belgian king, 1835–1909). King Leopold's daily breakfast consisted of six poached eggs, an enormous number of slices of toast, and an entire jar of marmalade.

Levasseur, Thérèse (French seamstress, 1721–1801). The common-law wife of Jean-Jacques Rousseau, Levasseur never knew which day of the week it was and never learned to tell the time. She has a mountain in Alaska named after her.

Leverton, Edith Waldemar (English writer, twentieth century). In her 1903 book *Small Homes And How To Furnish Them*, Mrs Waldemar Leverton explained how to decorate an ottoman: 'An idea which will appeal to those who have a rooted aversion to superstition, and a love for things uncanny, is to have a centre panel of velveteen, red for preference, and eight yards of silk, either orange or a bright green. In and out among the folds of the drapery twist several Japanese snakes, with a spider and a beetle here and there to break the monotony . . . Next get a bare black bough, as light in weight as possible, and on one of the branches fix an owl; if you cannot obtain a Japanese feathered one, it is quite easy to make one out of crinkled paper, stuffed with wadding, and painted to taste, the chief thing necessary being a pair of fine glittering eyes. It should be about six or nine inches high. At the bottom of the velvet panel arrange a few lizards.'

Levin, Bernard (English writer, 1928–2004, also a refrigerator). *See* Tippett, Michael

Liberace, Wladziu Valentino (American pianist, 1919–87). At the outset of his career, Liberace performed under the macho stage name Walter Busterkeys. Later, rich and famous, he had a piano made out of thousands of tooth-picks. His younger brother was named Rudolph Valentino Liberace.

Lombroso, Cesare (Italian criminologist, 1835–1909). Lombroso's insights into criminal psychology were out-lined in a 1911 pamphlet, 'Criminal Man, According To The Classification Of Cesare Lombroso Briefly Summarised By His Daughter, Gina Lombroso-Ferrero'. In the case of an assault on a young girl, she wrote: 'The victim survived and was able to point out the criminal – an imbecile, afflicted with goitre, stammering, strabismus, hydrocephaly, trochocephaly, and plagiocephaly, with arms of disproportionate length, the son and grandson of drunkards, who confessed the double crime and entreated pardon for the "trifling offence" since he had always done his duty and swept the staircase, even on the day he committed the crime.'

Lotti, Margherita (Italian saint, known as Rita of Cascia, 1381–1457). On the day after her baptism, the parents of the future Saint Rita of Cascia noticed a swarm of white bees flying around her as she slept in her crib. The bees buzzed in and out of her mouth without causing her any harm or injury. This was taken to be a sign from God that the infant's future life would be marked by industry, virtue, and devotion. She is the patron saint of French pop singer Mireille Mathieu.

Louis XV (French king, 1710–74). Louis XV is credited with popularising the potato in France. 'For more than two centuries the use of this invaluable plant was vehemently opposed,' wrote John Timbs. 'At last, Louis XV wore a bunch of its flowers in the midst of his courtiers, and the consumption of the root became universal in France.'

Love, Hannah (English duck enthusiast, twenty-first century). Hannah Love was a spokeswoman for Duck Density, an organisation that ranked British universities on the density of ducks on their lakes, ponds, meres and other bodies of water. Duck Density defined ducks as 'birds that go on water'.

Lovecraft, H. P. (American writer, 1890–1937). In the early 1970s, tabloid newspaper the *Sun* enjoined its readers to

'Go thou to H. P. Lovecraft – and shudder!' A native of Providence, Rhode Island, Lovecraft remained there for most of his life. He spent a brief period in New York City, which he described in terms of unutterable loathing that could have come from one of his stories. In a letter to fellow writer Frank Belknap Long, Lovecraft wrote of a visit to Manhattan's Lower East Side: 'The organic things – Italo-Semitico-Mongoloid – inhabiting that awful cesspool could not by any stretch of the imagination be call'd human. They were monstrous and nebulous adumbrations of the pithecanthropoid and amoebal; vaguely moulded from some stinking viscous slime of earth's corruption, and slithering and oozing in and on the filthy streets or in and out of windows and doorways in a fashion suggestive of nothing but infesting worms or deep-sea unnamabilities. They – or the degenerate gelatinous fermentation of which they were composed – seem'd to ooze, seep and trickle thro' the gaping cracks in the horrible houses . . and I thought of some avenue of Cyclopean and unwholesome vats, crammed to the vomiting-point with gangrenous vileness, and about to burst and inundate the world in one leprous cataclysm of semi-fluid rottenness. From that nightmare of perverse infection I could not carry away the memory of any living face. The individually grotesque was lost in the collectively devastating; which left on the eye only the broad, phantasmal lineaments of the morbid mould of disintegration and decay . . a yellow and leering mask with sour, sticky, acid ichors oozing at eyes, ears, nose and mouth, and abnormally bubbling from monstrous and unbelievable sores at every point.'

Luckner, Udo (Swedish hierophant, 1927–86). Believing that the vanished explorer Percy Fawcett had discovered a portal to a new dimension in Roncador, Brazil, Luckner established a sect called the Magical Nucleus in 1968. He dressed in a long white robe and a pointy hat emblazoned with the Star of David, and forbade members of the sect from eating meat or wearing jewellery. Failing to find the portal, Luckner decreed the world would end in 1982 and prepared his followers to descend into the hollow earth. After New Year's Day 1983, the Magical Nucleus gradually disbanded. *See* Nichols, Nichelle

Lutyens, Sir Edwin (English architect, 1869–1944). Lutyens was averse to long-stemmed glasses, fish-knives, cut flowers, silk lampshades, pile carpets, the seaside, statistics, painted nails, the diagonal placing of furniture and religious enthusiasm. *See* Wells, H. G.

Lynd, Robert (Irish writer, 1879–1949). Among Lynd's books was *The Pleasures Of Ignorance*, and among the things of which he confessed ignorance were moles. 'Who alive, for instance, knows all the moles of Sussex?', he asked. 'I confess I got my first sight of one a few days ago, and, though I had seen dead moles hanging from trees and had read descriptions of moles, the living creature was as unexpected as if one had come on it silent upon a peak in Darien.'

Macbeth, Lady (Shakespearean character, 1606). The actress Ellen Terry described Lady Macbeth as 'a delicate little creature with hypersensitive nerves'.

Machen, Arthur (Welsh writer, 1863–1947). Machen believed we are much mistaken if we think that there is, in ultimate reality, any such thing as a cow. *See* Matti, Franziska

Malthus, Thomas (English clergyman and political economist, 1766–1834). Of the author of *An Essay On The Principle Of Population*, Walter Bagehot wrote: 'There is nothing in Mr Malthus's life which is worth mentioning'.

Manning, Olivia (English novelist, 1908–80). At a party, John Gielgud knelt at the feet of Olivia Manning and told her he wanted to pay homage to her literary genius. Her reply was to moan that she could not hear a word he was saying because the party was far too noisy. She hated most other writers and had a particular animus against Iris Murdoch, because she 'looked as if she cut her own hair with a hacksaw'.

Mansfield, Katherine (New Zealand writer, 1888–1923). Suffering from tuberculosis, Katherine Mansfield hoped for a cure by going to stay at G. I. Gurdjieff's Institute for the Harmonious Development of Man in Fontainebleau. She arrived in October 1922. The guru and one-time carpet salesman had her chopping up carrots in the middle of the night and sleeping, when he allowed her to sleep, in a loft above the cow-barn, reasoning that the heady stench of gathered cows would benefit her. She was dead by January.

Mao Tse-tung (Chinese Communist Party Chairman, 1893–1976). Mao never brushed his teeth nor took a bath or shower. When he became grubby, a factotum was employed to rub him down with hot towels.

Martens, Wilfried (Belgian politician, 1936–2013). Martens pointed out that 'you can't say "I'll try to think like a Belgian." You either have it or you haven't.'

Martineau, Harriet (English writer and social theorist, 1802–76). So terrified was Harriet Martineau by the prospect of premature burial that she gave her doctor ten pounds as advance payment for the amputation of her head before interment.

Mary (Blessed Virgin, Mother of Christ, *c.* 18 BC–*c.* AD 41). In 2009, the Vatican issued helpful guidance for those who see a vision of the Virgin Mary: 'Anyone who claims to have seen an apparition [of Mary] will only be believed as long as they remain silent and do not court publicity over their claims. If they refuse to obey, this will be taken as a sign that their claims are false. The visionaries will then be visited by a team of psychiatrists, either atheists or Catholics, to certify their mental health while

theologians will assess the content of any heavenly messages to see if they contravene Church teachings. If the visionary is considered credible they will ultimately be questioned by one or more demonologists and exorcists to exclude the possibility that Satan is hiding behind the apparitions in order to deceive the faithful.'

Mathers, Moina (Swiss-Polish-English-Irish artist and occultist, 1865–1928). Mathers, the sister of philosopher Henri Bergson, was accused eighteen months after her death of killing Miss Netta Fornario by black magic. It was said Moina's spirit had appeared in the form of a monster cat and attacked the unfortunate Netta. However, the scratches on the corpse were more likely the result of running naked in the dark over rough country, which Miss Fornario had been doing immediately before her collapse.

Matti, Franziska (Swiss animal communication expert, twenty-first century). When a cow named Yvonne went missing in Bavaria in 2011, those concerned for her welfare were grateful to Franziska Matti, who was in telepathic communication with her. 'I spoke to [Yvonne] yesterday and she said that she was fine but didn't feel ready to come out of hiding. She said she knew that Ernst had been waiting for her but that she was scared. She said she thought that humans would lock her up and she would no longer be free.' Ernst was a bull with 'a deep baritone moo'. Yvonne was eventually found and taken to a cow sanctuary. *See* Stein, Gertrude

Maxwell-Lefroy, Harold (English entomologist and founder of Rentokil, 1877–1925). Maxwell-Lefroy choked to death on a gas insecticide of his own invention. His last words were 'the little beggars got the best of me this time!'

Mazarin, Duc (French soldier and nobleman, 1642–1713). Mazarin had a series of visions which convinced him he was a tulip. He thus instructed his servants to dig a hole in his garden, plant him in it, and empty watering-cans over his head.

McAlpine, Alistair (English jack of all trades, 1942–2014). McAlpine was variously a property developer, political fixer, pearl farmer, shopkeeper, art gallery owner, writer and bed and breakfast proprietor. The one constant in his life was a love of collecting, and he amassed splendid collections of, among other things, fine art, medieval African beads, snowdrops, and police truncheons.

McCartney, Paul (English Beatle, b. 1942). In 1964, McCartney and his fellow Beatles were banned from performing in Israel. An official government investigation into the moptops had discovered compelling evidence that their 'yeah-yeah-yeah howls are capable of striking dead a real beetle'.

Menken, Adah Isaacs (American actress, painter and poet, 1835–68). So famous was Adah Menken in her hey-day that she was known simply as 'the Menken'. Her popularity was so great that she had a triumph as Lady Macbeth in spite of her ignorance of the play, the character, and, indeed, her lines. But the critics were not kind to *Infelicia*, her debut volume of poetry. *The Athenaeum* called it 'a wilderness of rubbish and affected agonies of yearnings after the unspeakable, which achieve the non-sensical', while *The Saturday Review* described it as 'a bleared panorama of deaths and sighs and blood and tears and fire and general gloom and watery ghastliness'.

Menken hoped to improve the book's chances by putting about a rumour that the verses were actually written by her friend Algernon Charles Swinburne.

Merced, José (American voodooist, twenty-first century). Merced, a devotee of Santeria voodoo, went to court in 2009 to challenge the authorities in Euless, Texas. They had used health and safety laws to stop him practising an essential part of his religion. 'To be clear,' said counsel for the town, 'Merced does not want to sacrifice a goat in his home. He wants to sacrifice five to seven goats, one to two turtles, one duck, ten to fourteen chickens, five to seven guinea hens, and ten to fourteen doves all at one time. Keeping and killing that many animals in a residential neighbourhood poses disease transmission dangers. It creates stench and filth, is repulsive, and has no place in an urban environment.' The judges noted that Santeria centres around spirits called orishas, which are divine representatives of Olodumare, the supreme deity. Santeria rituals seek to engage these orishas, honour them, and encourage their involvement in the material world. Doing so requires the use of life energy, or ashé, the highest concentration of which is found in animal blood. Merced won his case. *See* Zardari, Asif Ali

Meredith, George (English writer, 1828–1909). In the Christmas 1896 issue of the *Saturday Review*, Sir Max Beerbohm published *The Victory Of Aphasia Ghibberish*, a parody of George Meredith: 'In the heart of insular Cosmos, remote by some scores of leagues of hodge-trod arable or pastoral – not more than half a snuff-pinch to gaping tourists' nostrils accustomed to inhalation of prairie-winds, but enough for perspective – from these marginal sands, trident-scraped, we are to fancy, by a helmeted Dame Abstract, familiarly profiled on discs of current bronze, price of a loaf for humbler maws disdainful of Gallic side-dishes for the titillation of choicer palates, stands Ghibberish Park, a house of some pretensions, mentioned at Runnymede, with the spreading exception of wings given to it in latter times by Daedelean monsters not to be balked of billiards or traps for Terpsichore, and owned for unbroken generations by a healthy line of procreant Ghibberishes, to the undoing of collateral branches eager for the birth of a female.' According to the critic F. E. Baily, 'This is by no means an exaggeration of Meredith's style. In fact, anyone who has struggled with the opening chapters of *One Of Our Conquerors* might describe it as an understatement.'

Messiah of Gévaudan (French Messiah, sixth century). Gregory of Tours in his *Chronicles* relates the story of a man who was driven insane by flies in a forest near Arles. Two years later, in 591, he appeared in Gévaudan, dressed in animal pelts and announcing he was Christ. He soon had an army of a thousand followers, and sent naked somersaulting emissaries to Bishop Aurelius in Le Puy. The bishop perceived the Devil at work. When the Messiah arrived, the Bishop's henchmen dragged him to the ground and stabbed him to death. Some twelve centuries later, Gévaudan was overrun by packs of man-eating wolf-like creatures, but that may be coincidental.

Metternich, Klemens von (Austrian statesman, 1773–1859). On a visit to England, Metternich was served rhubarb tart, and was so delighted with it that he had plants sent to grow in his Austrian garden. At a large and important state dinner the following year, he told his cook to serve the rhubarb as a dessert. The cook 'knew nothing of English usages, and, selecting the large leaves, served them up as a spinach. The guests made wry faces at this English dish, and well they might; and rhubarb was from that time discarded from the Prince's table.'

Millin, Bill (Scottish bagpiper, 1922–2010). Millin was the personal piper to Lord Lovat and in that capacity took part in the D-Day landings. Unarmed apart from a ceremonial dagger tucked into his sock, he began piping as soon as he disembarked from the landing craft, and then strolled up and down the beach playing 'Highland Laddie' and other tunes. Later, German soldiers who had been taken prisoner told him they had not shot him because they thought he had gone off his head.

Miró, Joan (Spanish artist, 1893–1983). Miró was a keen boxer, and once had a fight with Ernest Hemingway, who claimed to be earning his living as a professional sparring partner. The difference in their heights meant that Miró 'only came up to his belly-button', as he put it. 'It was rather comical,' he added, 'there was a real ring, and all around in the stands, a crowd of homosexuals.'

Mobutu, Joseph-Désiré (Congolese politician and President, 1930–97). When he changed his country's name to Zaire in 1971, Mobutu also changed his own name to Mobutu Sese Seko Kuku Ngbendu Wa Za Banga, which translates as 'the all powerful warrior who, because of his endurance and inflexible will to win, shall go from conquest to conquest, leaving fire in his wake'.

Moore, Marianne (American poet, 1887–1972). The Ford motor company hired Marianne Moore to devise names for their cars. She suggested Mongoose Civique, Resilient Bullet, Silver Sword, Varsity Stroke, Pastelogram, Andante con Moto, and Utopian Turtletop. None of these were used, and the company decided to call their new model the Edsel.

More, Hannah (English writer, 1745–1833). Hannah More aimed to counter the 'infection' caused by the supply of vulgar and licentious chapbooks by issuing her own Cheap Repository Tracts. These contained stories of 'Striking Conversions, Holy Lives, Happy Deaths, Providential Deliverances, Judgements on the Breakers of Commandments, Stories of Good and Wicked Apprentices, Hardened Sinners, Pious Servants &c.' They all had happy endings, the moral being that everything turns out for the best if you go to church and observe the Sabbath.

Morley, Robert (English actor, 1908–92). When the time came for his son Sheridan to go to school, Morley placed an advertisement in *The Times*: 'Father with horrible memories of his own schooldays at Wellington is searching for a school for his son where the food matters as much as the education, and the standards are those of a good three-star seaside hotel'. Sheridan duly attended Sizewell in Suffolk, run by a fat Quaker who had trained as a master chef before opening the school.

Morse, Samuel (American inventor, 1791–1872). Morse was, naturally enough, the first man to send a message by Morse Code. It read: 'What hath God wrought?'

Motion, Andrew (English poet, b. 1952). Motion summons the poetic Muse by drinking Lemsip, which tricks his brain into feeling slightly ill and self-pitying.

Mowbray, Jay Henry (American writer, twentieth century). Mowbray was the author of the 1912 book *Sinking Of The 'Titanic', Most Appalling Ocean Horror With Graphic Descriptions Of Hundreds Swept To Eternity Beneath The Waves; Panic Stricken Multitude Facing Sure Death, And Thrilling Stories Of This Most Overwhelming Catastrophe To Which Is Added Vivid Accounts Of Heart-Rending Scenes, When Hundreds Were Doomed To Watery Graves, Compiled From Soul Stirring Stories Told By Eye Witnesses Of This Terrible Horror Of The Briny Deep.*

Muggleton, Lodowicke (English Muggletonian, 1609–98). In 1652 Muggleton and his cousin John Reeve received a commission from God, who told them they were the two witnesses referred to in *Revelations* 11:3. They were empowered to pronounce upon the fate of individuals and to curse for all eternity those so deserving – such as Scotsmen, for whom Muggleton had a pathological loathing. They gathered followers and formed a sect. Muggletonians believed that human reason was unclean, and this led them to reject physical science. They refused to accept the laws of gravity or the rules of mathematics, and they considered astronomy to be wrong. The stars, they said, were only as big as God made them appear from earth. In later years, Muggletonians banned hot air ballooning, because the balloons would crash into the sky, a solid band around the earth. Other than the Quakers, the Muggletonians were the only sect that sprang up in the foment of the English Civil War to survive into the twentieth century. In the 1970s, one Philip Noakes came to light in Kent, a living Muggletonian in possession of a huge archive of material covering their entire history. *See* Scott, Sir Walter

Mura, Corinna (American singer, *c.* 1909–65). Corinna Mura was immortalised on screen when she defiantly sang 'La Marseillaise' with guitar accompaniment in Rick's Bar in the film *Casablanca*. She was the stepmother of the illustrator Edward Gorey (q.v.).

Musonius (Roman philosopher, 20?–101?) The teacher of Epictetus, Gaius Musonius Rufus taught, among other things, that it was shameful for people to wear gloves – or, as he put it, 'soft and hairy coverings'.

Mussolini, Benito (Italian statesman, 1883–1945). Mussolini had a terror of moonlight touching his face when he was asleep.

Muybridge, Eadweard (English photographer, 1830–1904). Muybridge's wife bore a son, Florado Helios. When Muybridge discovered he was not the father, and that the child had been sired by a notorious confidence-trickster named George Harry Larkins, he tracked Larkins down and shot him dead. In spite of admitting the murder, Muybridge was acquitted. One of his favourite snacks was maggot-riddled cheese.

Mytton, John (English rake, 1796–1834). 'Mad Jack' Mytton was scion of a family which dated its nobility back to the Plantagenets. His father died when he was eighteen months old, and he inherited a vast estate with a huge annual income. By the time he died in debtors' prison at the age of thirty-eight, the estate had been sold and he was penniless. Mytton enjoyed going on winter duck hunts stripped to the waist or completely naked, lying in snowdrifts awaiting his prey. Once, when he had hiccups, he cured them by setting fire to the shirt he was wearing. His death was ascribed to 'disease of the brain'.

Naipaul, V. S. (Trinidadian writer, b. 1932). Naipaul hates the word 'Scandinavian', which he considers 'full of ice and death and sullen coitus'.

Nami, Mohammad Hassan (Iranian general and politician, twenty-first century). After his appointment as Communications and Technology Minister in the Iranian government, Nami announced plans for 'Basir', an Islamic version of Google Earth. 'We are developing this service with the Islamic views we have in Iran and we will put a kind of information on our website that would take people of the world towards reality. Our values in Iran are the values of God and this would be the difference between Basir and the Google Earth, which belongs to the ominous triangle of the United States, England, and the Zionists.'

Napoleon (French Emperor, 1769–1821). Napoleon's handwriting was such an illegible scrawl that the letters he sent from Germany to the Empress Joséphine were at first thought to be roughly-sketched maps.

Nazário de Lima, Ronaldo Luís (Brazilian footballer, b. 1976). During a football match in 2009, referring to a footballer named Rolando, a television commentator wondered 'how long is it since Ronaldo was marked by an anagram of himself?'

Nerval, Gérard de (French writer, 1808–55). De Nerval had a pet lobster named Thibault which he used to take on walks through the Palais Royal gardens in Paris on the end of a blue silk ribbon. Challenged to explain this eccentricity, he replied: 'And what could be quite so ridiculous as making a dog, a cat, a gazelle, a lion or any other beast follow one about? I have affection for lobsters. They are tranquil, serious and they know the secrets of the sea.'

Newbolt, Henry (English poet, 1862–1938). In 1911, Newbolt, together with W. B. Yeats, travelled to Thomas Hardy's home in Dorset to present the novelist with a gold medal from the Royal Society for Literature. Expecting to find a large gathering to celebrate the occasion, they were disconcerted to find just Hardy and his wife, who by this time hated each other. Throughout the ensuing dinner, Emma Hardy sat in stony silence with a cat perched on either side of her plate, and by the end of the evening, Newbolt recalled, 'We were no longer in the world of our waking lives.'

Newcomb, Harvey (American writer, nineteenth century). In *A Practical Directory For Young Christian Females* (1851), Newcomb issued a stern warning: 'I cannot see how a Christian, who has had a taste of "angel's food", can relish the miserable trash contained in novels. The tendency of novel reading is most pernicious. It enervates the mental powers, and unfits them for close study and serious contemplation. It dissipates the mind, and creates a diseased imagination. It promotes a sickly sensibility, and renders its votaries unfit for the pursuits of real life. It is a great waste of time, and on this account alone may be regarded as sinful.'

Newton, Sir Isaac (English physicist and mathematician, 1642–1727). In 1689, Newton was elected Member of Parliament for Cambridge University. He held the post for one year, during which time he spoke only once – asking someone to close the windows, as he could feel a cold draught.

Nichols, Nichelle (American actress, b. 1932). Playing Lt. Uhura in *Star Trek* was not Nichols' only connection with outer space. Her brother Thomas was a long-time member of the Heaven's Gate cult, the followers of Marshall Herff Applewhite ('Do') and Bonnie Lu Nettles ('Ti') who hoped to join a spaceship trailing in the wake of the Hale-Bopp comet in 1997. The group committed mass suicide when the comet passed.

Nico (German singer, 1938–88, real name Christa Päffgen). Sepulchral of voice, purveyor of unremitting Teutonic gloom and heroin addict, Nico could not have had a more inappropriate death. Rather than expiring in some edgy urban drug-den, she suffered a fatal topple from her bike while cycling in the bright sunshine of a seaside resort.

Nixon, Richard Milhous (American politician and POTUS, 1913–94). One of Nixon's favourite pastimes was mashing potatoes.

Niyazov, Saparmurat (Turkmenistani dictator, 1940–2006). Under Niyazov's rule, the existing names of airports, towns, days of the week, and months of the year were abolished and replaced by his own name or those of members of his family. April, for example, was given his mother's name. He also named a meteor after himself, and, as if that were not enough, ensured that the names when written were inscribed in an entirely new alphabet of his own devising, to replace Cyrillic. He banned beards, car radios, and lip-synching in films. His volume of poetry was required reading for all citizens. He died not long after replacing all the country's doctors with untrained conscripts and replacing the Hippocratic Oath with a pledge of allegiance to himself.

Obama, Barack (American politician and POTUS, b. 1961). Obama keeps an Egg of Power on his desk in the Oval Office. *See* Orwell, George

O'Connor, Philip (English writer, 1916–98). O'Connor was an *habitué* of 1930s Fitzrovia known for speaking in cryptograms, spoonerisms and jingles, delivering sentences backwards and falling about drunk. After standing behind a door and saying 'Boo!' to T. S. Eliot, he briefly became notorious as The Man Who Stood Behind The Door And Said 'Boo!' To T. S. Eliot. In the 1950s he was the partner of the future *EastEnders* soap opera actress Anna Wing.

Odd Family, The (English oddbods, seventeenth–eighteenth century). A nineteenth-century history of Ipswich relates that 'in the reign of William III, there resided at Ipswich a family which, from the number of peculiarities belonging to it, was distinguished by the name of "the Odd Family". Every event remarkably good or bad happened to this family on an odd day of the month, and every member had something odd in his or her person, manner, or behaviour. The very letters in their Christian names always happened to be an odd number; the husband's name was Peter, and the wife's name Raboh: they had seven children, all boys, viz, Solomon, Roger, James, Matthew, Jonas, David and Ezekiel. The husband had but one leg, his wife but one arm. Solomon was born blind of one eye, and Roger lost his sight by accident. James had his left ear bit off by a boy in a quarrel, and Matthew was born with only three fingers on his right hand. Jonas had a stump foot and David was hump-backed. All these, except the latter, were remarkably short, while Ezekiel was six foot one inch high at the age of nineteen. The stump-footed Jonas and the hump-backed David got wives of fortune, but no girls in the borough would listen to the addresses of their brothers. The husband's hair was as black as jet, and the wife's remarkably white; yet every one of the children's hair was red. The husband was killed by accidentally falling into a deep pit in the year 1701; and his wife, refusing all kinds of sustenance, died five days after him, and they were buried in one grave. In 1703, Ezekiel enlisted as a grenadier; and although he was afterwards wounded in twenty-three places, he recovered. Roger, James, Matthew, Jonas and David, it appears by the church registers, died in different places and were buried on the same day, in 1713; and Solomon and Ezekiel were drowned together in crossing the Thames in the year 1723. Such a collection of odd circumstances never occurred before in one family.'

O'Donnell, Elliott (Irish writer and ghost hunter, 1872–1965). If his 1934 book *Strange Cults And Secret Societies Of Modern London* is to be believed, O'Donnell gathered most of his material from chance encounters with strangers in pubs. Over a pint, they would divulge details of hitherto hidden shenanigans in the metropolis. One such account tells of a man who, staggering home drunk one evening, 'by some means he could never quite explain, got into a strange house instead of his own, and found himself in a semi-dark room full of queer-looking people, male and female, clad in leopard skins. Being given a skin by a dark, foreign-looking girl, he tried to put it on and, in spite of his addled senses, he so far succeeded that no one appeared to notice it was upside down. Probably no one paid any heed to him, everyone's attention being centred on a woman, who was standing in the middle of the room, haranguing them. My friend could not see her very distinctly owing to the lights being turned down, but he judged her to be coloured, she looked so dark, and not a British subject, as she spoke with a decided foreign accent. The cool night air, blowing into the room, through an open window near at hand, gradually sobered him, and his brain became quite clear. He realised then that the people around him belonged to some strange exotic cult, and finally the amazing fact that they were Leopard and Panther People dawned on him.'

Olivier, Laurence (English actor, 1907–89). Olivier said in an interview that the sweet smell of success 'smells just like Brighton and oyster-bars and things like that'.

Ono, Yoko (Japanese artist, musician, and Beatle-wife, b. 1933). *See* Cardew, Cornelius

Ormerod, Edward Latham (English physician, 1819–73). John Ruskin declared that Ormerod's *History Of Wasps* (actually entitled *British Social Wasps*) ought to be a standard book in the primary education of girls.

Orton, Joe (English playwright, 1933–67). Orton's mother died in December 1966 while his play *Loot* was being staged. When he returned from the funeral in Leicester, Orton brought with him her false teeth, and took them to the theatre. He recorded in his diary: 'I said to Kenneth Cranham, "Here. I thought you'd like the originals." He said "What?" "Teeth," I said. "Whose?" he said. "My mum's," I said. He looked very sick. "You see," I said, "it's obvious that you're not thinking of the events of the play in terms of reality if a thing affects you like that." Simon Ward shook like a jelly when I gave them to him.'

Orwell, George (English writer, real name Eric Blair, 1903–50). The diaries of important literary figures, particularly those as politically engaged as Orwell, are a goldmine for the historian. A year before Europe was engulfed in the Second World War, here is Orwell writing in his journal (the entries for each day are complete and unabridged):

21.11.38– Two eggs.
22.11.38– Two eggs.
25.11.38– Two eggs.
27.11.38– One egg.
28.11.38– Two eggs.
29.11.38– One egg.
30.11.38– Two eggs.
4.12.38– Two eggs.
6.12.38– Two eggs. Nights now are distinctly chilly.
10.12.38– One egg.
11.12.38– Two eggs.
13.12.38– Two eggs.
18.12.38– Two eggs.
21.12.38– Two eggs. Finer, cool, a few spots of rain. One of the pigeons is dead – cause unknown.

26-28.12.38– Have been ill. Not certain about number of eggs, but about 9.

Oswald, Lee Harvey (American schoolbook depository worker and assassin, 1939–63). To avert the probability of his grave being desecrated by people unhinged by the killing of President Kennedy, Oswald was buried under the name 'William Bobo'. *See* Ruby, Jack

Ovda (Finno-Ugric evil spirit). Ovda dwells in chasms, forests and ruins of old castles. It appears as either a man or a woman with feet backwards. It can be heard to laugh and clap its hands. It entices people to wrestle and then tickles them to death. If touched under the left arm it becomes powerless.

Ovid (Roman poet, 43 BC–AD 17/18). In Ancient Rome, William Bodham Donne tells us, 'Sometimes the fine gentleman, who declined taking an active part in public affairs, found himself unexpectedly a thousand miles from home, with an imperial rescript in his portmanteau enjoining him not to return to Rome without special leave. To such a compulsory journey was the poet Ovid condemned, apparently for his very particular attentions to the Princess Julia. His exile was a piece of ingenious cruelty. He was sent to Tomi, which was far beyond the range of all fashionable bathing-places. The climate was atrocious; the neighbourhood was worse; the wine was execrable and was often hard frozen, and eaten like a lozenge, and his only society was that of the barracks, or a few rich but unpolished corn-factors. To write verses from morn to dewy eve was the unfortunate poet's only solace; and he sent so many reams of elegies to Rome, that his friends came at last to vote him a bore, and he was reduced, for want of fitting audience, to learn the Getic language, and read his lachrymose couplets to circles of gaping barbarians.'

Palladino, Eusapia (Italian spiritualist medium, 1854–1918). Eusapia Palladino claimed that when she was a baby she was dropped on her head causing a hole to be made in her skull. This was the cranial opening through which a cool breeze would issue when she went into a trance. Her séances were often accompanied by violent muscular twitchings, screaming and shouting. A newspaper report described her as a 'coarse-looking woman of the Latin type' who, when anyone doubted her genuineness, 'shrieks and gets very excited'.

Palmer, William (English doctor, the Prince of Poisoners, 1824–56). Some years after the poisoner Palmer was hanged for murder, a London publisher brought out a book in which the entire trial transcript, together with an account of Palmer's sporting activities, was translated into Ancient Greek.

Paracelsus (Swiss-German natural philosopher, real name Philippus Aureolus Theophrastus Bombastus Von Hohenheim, 1493–1541). Paracelsus kept a small avian devil imprisoned in the pommel of his sword. He also coined the word 'zinc', and made the first recorded homunculus from a bag of bones, sperm, skin fragments and animal hair, these ingredients laid in the ground surrounded by horse manure for forty days, at which point the embryo formed.

Paterson, Owen (English politician, b. 1956). As the government minister responsible for the British badger cull of 2013, Paterson was asked why it had been ineffective. 'The badgers moved the goalposts,' he replied.

Patridge, Sylvester (English astrologer, eighteenth century). Patridge took space in *Poor Robin's Almanac* in 1733 to advertise his services: 'The best time to cut hair. How moles and dreams are to be interpreted. When most proper season to bleed. Under what aspect of the moon best to draw teeth, and cut corns. Pairing of nails, on what day unlucky. What the kindest sign to graft or inoculate in; to open bee-hives, and kill swine. How many hours boiling my Lady Kent's pudding requires. With other notable questions, fully and faithfully resolved, by me Sylvester Patridge, student in physic and astrology, near the Gun in Moorfields. Of whom likewise may be had, at reasonable rates, trusses, antidotes, elixirs, love-powders. Washes for freckles, plumpers, glass-eyes, false calves and noses, ivory-jaws, and a new receipt to turn red hair into black.'

Patterson, George W. (American variety artist, nineteenth/twentieth century). In January 1900, *The Strand* magazine reported on Patterson's thrilling variety act. 'A curious and ingenious method of entertaining the public by the aid of electricity has been introduced by Mr George W. Patterson, of Chicago. This gentleman has devised a means of swinging electrically lighted Indian clubs in such a way as to produce startling, yet beautiful, spectacular effects. Although this kind of electrical display with Indian clubs is entirely new so far as the public is concerned, Mr Patterson has given much time and thought to the subject, and his entertainments have not reached their present degree of excellence and novelty without a great deal of patient study of that vast and marvellous subject which we call electricity.'

Pavlova, Anna (Russian ballerina, 1881–1931). Pavlova had a pet swan named Jack. *See* Henman, Tim

Peary, Robert (American explorer, 1856–1920). Peary had idiosyncratic views on how best to survive the harsh polar climate. On his expeditions, he never slept in a tent, preferring to remain out in the open with his dogs. He chewed frozen chunks of pemmican (concentrated fat and protein) rather than cooking it.

Penn, William (English Quaker, founder of Pennsylvania, 1644–1718). When Lodowicke Muggleton (q.v.) published a tract entitled *The Neck Of The Quakers Broken* in 1663, Penn took a leaf out of the Muggletonians' book and pronounced a curse upon Muggleton himself: 'To the bottomless pit are you sentenced, from whence you came, and where the endless worm shall gnaw and torture your imaginary soul to eternity.'

Persimmon (English racehorse, nineteenth century). In 1896, a horse called Persimmon won the Derby. It was no ordinary horse, for its owner was the Prince of Wales, later Edward VII. The *Daily Telegraph* reported the scene following its win: 'In superabundant gratification at this right Royal triumph, all conventionality was thrown to the

141

winds. Hats rose in the air, sticks and umbrellas were cast away as mere bagatelles; and, with a marvellous decision of instinct, the huge throng broke in on the course, turned with one smiling, happy, radiant face towards the Royal box, and delivered such volleys of cheers as have never before, and probably never will again, be heard. There was no class distinction in this great demonstration. The aristocratic patrons of the Club enclosure were not differently constituted to the common clay. They cheered and cheered again, while the greater outside public waxed positively wild in raptures of enthusiasm. Persimmon won magnificently; and the victory will go down to posterity with a halo of triumph. Henry V revelled in the memory of St Crispian's Day; but who will say that an equal meed of glory will not attach to the day of St Simon's gallant descendant?'

Person, Waverly (American seismologist, b. 1925). In a spectacular example of nominative determinism, Waverly Person is an expert seismologist often consulted by the media to comment on earthquakes and tsunamis.

Pert, Henry (English archer, d. 1552). Pert, a Nottinghamshire gentleman, managed to shoot himself in the head with his own bow and arrow in 1552. Intending to aim the arrow directly up into the air, he drew the bow back to its full extent. The arrow became caught, so he lowered the bow and leaned over to take a peek at the problem, at which point the arrow came free and penetrated his head. He died the following day.

Peter the Great (Russian Tsar, 1672–1725). The diarist John Evelyn was a keen gardener and was especially proud of the holly hedges at his property in Deptford. He was distraught, therefore, when Peter the Great came to stay. The Tsar was ostensibly in London to study ship-building on the Thames, but he preferred to throw drunken parties, during which he would climb into a wheelbarrow and have a servant propel him at speed through Evelyn's flowerbeds and hedges.

Philby, Kim (English spy, 1912–88). The journalist Charles Wheeler (late father-in-law of Boris Johnson) was asked if he was surprised when he learned of Philby's treachery. 'Not really,' said Wheeler, 'I never really trusted him. He was the sort of fellow who . . . smiled at breakfast, that sort of thing.'

Philip, Duke of Edinburgh (British royal consort, b. 1921). The people of Tanna in Vanuatu worship Prince Philip as a god. There is an ancient story about the son of a mountain spirit venturing across the seas to look for a powerful woman to marry. At some point in the fifties the islanders put two and two together and worked out that this must be the Duke of Edinburgh. He acknow-ledges their devotion and occasionally sends them copies of his official portrait.

Picasso, Pablo (Spanish artist, 1881–1973). Picasso loved fast cars but never learned to drive. Nor did he ever learn to swim.

143

Pierce, George Winslow (American writer, 1841–1917). Pierce's 1891 book, *My Soundspeed Discovery, Expanding into a Constructive Medley of Wit and Song; being a Four Years After-Inflorescence of The Life-Romance of an Algebraist*, was lauded with praise, printed as blurb on the second edition. It was described as a book like no other that ever will be, scintillating, fascinating, subtle, sincere, sublime, gorgeous, fantastic, exquisite, ambrosial, most soul-compelling, so suggestive of still higher things, a glimpse into Eleusinian mysteries or the literature of the planet Mars, like purple mountain peaks rising above the clouds and disappearing in the whiteness of shrouds of mist. The man who taught Pierce at Harvard added, 'The ebullition of your thoughts makes me feel as if I had been attracted to within a few hundred miles of the sun and had his gas-jets in full view.' Among Pierce's other publications was *Four fifths of Goldsmith's Deserted Village, the other one fifth without loss or injury to the sense having been expunged.*

Pierrepoint, Albert (English hangman, 1905–92). After retiring as England's chief executioner, Pierrepoint opened a pub in Lancashire called 'Help The Poor Struggler'. Always fond of the ladies, he once sang love songs over the telephone to the actress Diana Dors.

Pimbley, Arthur Francis (American heraldry expert, twentieth century). Pimbley self-published his *Dictionary of Heraldry* in 1908. An example of the useful information it provides is the definition given for 'barry bendy dexter and sinister', to wit 'a combination of barry and bendy dexter and sinister'.

144

Pining, Dietrich (German pirate, *c.* 1430–91). Together with his fellow pirate Hans Pothorst (q.v.), Pining may have been the first European to make landfall in the New World. On their voyages, the pair often sailed to Greenland to avoid the attentions of Danes trying to put a stop to their piratical ways. On one occasion, sixteen years before Columbus's discovery, it is thought they accidentally blundered ashore in Labrador. It is for this reason that some people insist on referring to America as Pining & Pothorst Land.

Pitt, William, the Elder (English statesman, 1708–78). Ageing, sick, and half-mad at the time of the American Revolutionary War, Pitt let it be known that he wanted to be called 'the scarecrow of violence'.

Pius XII (Italian Pope, 1876–1958). For Pius XII, papal infallibility extended far beyond matters of Roman Catholic doctrine. The former Cardinal Eugenio Pacelli considered himself an expert on a vast range of subjects. Groups of visitors to the Vatican would be regaled with lectures (or 'allocutions') on topics including dentistry, gymnastics, gynaecology, aeronautics, cinematography, psychology, psychiatry, agriculture, plastic surgery, newscasting and gas central heating. When T. S. Eliot was granted a private audience in 1948, Pius took the opportunity to explain literature to him.

Pliny The Elder (Roman natural philosopher, 23–79). In his *Natural History*, Pliny recommended beating parrots about the head with iron bars to shut them up. Their heads are as hard as their beaks, he claimed, and any lesser violence will fail to stop their gabbling.

Poe, Edgar Allan (American writer, 1809–49). Poe's dying words were 'Reynolds! Reynolds! Reynolds!' He was calling out for Jeremiah Reynolds, an enthusiastic supporter of the hollow earth theory of John Cleeve Symmes (q.v.), one of the inspirations for *The Narrative Of Arthur Gordon Pym Of Nantucket*. Reynolds was not present at Poe's deathbed.

Politianus, Angelus (Italian scholar and poet, 1454–94). Sir John Hawkins tells us that Politianus, or Politian, 'who passed for the finest wit of his time in Italy, met with a fate which punished his criminal love. Being professor of eloquence at Florence, he unhappily became enamoured of one of his young scholars who was of an illustrious family, but whom he could neither corrupt by his great presents, nor by the force of his eloquence. The vexation he conceived at this disappointment was so great as to throw him into a burning fever; and in the violence of the fit he made two couplets of a song upon the object with which he was transported. He had no sooner done this than he raised himself from his bed, took his lute, and accompanied it with his voice in an air so tender and affecting that he expired in singing the second couplet.'

Pollock, Sir Frederick (English baronet, politician, and lawyer, 1783–1870). When Pollock was appointed Attorney General, he wrote to the College of Heralds asking how much they would charge to provide him with a suitable coat of arms. Upon receiving their quotation, he replied: 'My compliments to Garter-King-of-Arms, and tell him he may go to the devil, in flames gules, with a pitchfork argent stuck in his backside proper.'

Pop, Iggy (American musician, real name James Osterberg, b. 1947). At the time of recording the classic album *Raw Power* with the Stooges in London in 1972, Iggy Pop's drug of choice was neither heroin nor amphetamines but Harvey's Bristol Cream sherry.

Popper, Karl (Austrian-British philosopher, 1902–94). In 1946 Popper was invited to give a lecture at the London School of Economics at an event chaired by his fellow philosopher Ludwig Wittgenstein. Popper's paper was entitled 'Are There Philosophical Problems?' Wittgenstein, who thought the answer to the question was 'No', there being only linguistic games, grew increasingly exasperated and, armed with a poker, repeatedly brandished it as if to violently attack Popper. Eventually Wittgenstein challenged Popper to name a single moral principle. Popper (by his own account) replied: 'Not to threaten visiting lecturers with pokers.' Wittgenstein let fall the poker and stormed out.

Pothorst, Hans (German pirate, *c.* 1440–90). Some years after accidentally discovering Pining & Pothorst Land, Pothorst and his fellow pirate Pining (q.v.) settled on a rock called Hvitsark, some way off the coast of Iceland. According to Olaus Magnus, Archbishop of Uppsala, in his *Historia de gentibus septentrionalibus* (1555), 'they lived there outlawed with their fellow-rovers and inflicted many atrocities on every seafarer, whether sailing close at hand or at a distance'. They built a lead compass atop the rock to help them in determining the shortest direction to go in their 'profitable plundering forays'. The compass is depicted in the superb map of Scandinavia made by Olaus in 1539 and published in Ülm.

Potter, Stephen (English writer, 1900–69). Best known for his comic writing, Potter's literary output was wide-ranging. In 1930 he published the first critical appraisal of D. H. Lawrence. Unfortunately, it came out very shortly after Lawrence's death, and was thus seen, mistakenly, as a somewhat inadequate memorial. It also contained a misprint, rendering 'Sea And Sardinia' as 'Sex And Sardinia', which itself then became joked about as 'Sex And Sardines'. The misprint was perhaps inevitable, given that Potter's manuscripts were described as 'a mass of dirty bits of paper, vilely typed, corrected in illegible biro, episodic and half-revised'.

Powell, Willis J. (American horse-tamer, d. 1848). Some of Powell's horse-taming methods were summarised in *The Arabian Art Of Taming And Training Wild And Vicious Horses,* published in 1856. He recommended speaking to horses in Latin or Greek.

Powys, John Cowper (English writer, 1872–1963). Powys was extremely clumsy. Lighting a fire could take him up to two hours and result in holes burned in the carpet and a thick layer of ash over everything. He never worked out how to open a window or pull down a blind. His attempts at manoeuvering a tea tray were likened by one observer to the docking of the *Queen Mary*. On one occasion he ended up with his arm in a sling after an ill-advised attempt to clap his hands.

Presley, Reg (English musician and inventor, real name Reginald Ball, 1941–2013). In addition to being the lead singer of the Troggs, immortalised by their cover version of 'Wild Thing', Presley was an amateur inventor who patented an airport fog dispersal system. In later life he turned his attention to UFOs, crop circles and alien abductions.

Price, Harry (English psychic researcher, 1881–1948). The tireless psychic researcher Harry Price was the inventor of the telekinetoscope. This was a brass cup mounted on a metal tripod with levelling screws and had a turned-in flange. Around the periphery of the cup, stamped in the flange, were twelve small holes. Inside the cup was a contact-maker of thin sheet fibre connected with two brass strips to the leads of rubber and silk insulated flex. The whole was mounted on a rubber base. A narrow strip of thin metal was fastened around the contact-maker connecting by a piece of tin fuse-wire the brass screw holding the fibre slip. When the contact-maker was placed in the cup, a bubble composed of distilled water, glycerine and Castile soap was drawn across the top of the cup. To prevent accidental destruction of the bubble a glass shade was placed over the entire contraption, which in turn was put inside a metal cage to register – if possible – the presence of any psychic power.

Pulitzer, Joseph (Hungarian-American newspaper magnate, 1847–1911). In later life, when blind, Pulitzer became increasingly oversensitive to noise. The click of a spoon against a saucer, the gurgle of water poured into a glass, the striking of a match; these caused spasms of agony. He was most bitterly resentful when 'he came within hearing distance of ill-bred persons'. Aboard his yacht, he was able to exert greater control, and staff and crew wore rubber-soled shoes and were forbidden to eat almonds.

Radcliffe, Ann (English writer, 1764–1823). The author of *The Mysteries Of Udolpho,* Ann Radcliffe was one of the pioneers of the Gothic novel. Her works were described by Sir Walter Scott (q.v.) as follows: 'In the writings of Mrs Radcliffe there is a considerable degree of uniformity and mannerism. . . Her heroines too nearly resemble each other, or rather they possess hardly any shade of difference. They have all blue eyes and auburn hair – the form of each of them has 'the airy lightness of a nymph' – they are all fond of watching the setting sun, and catching the purple tints of evening, and the vivid glow or fading splendour of the western horizon. Unfortunately they are all likewise early risers. I say unfortunately, for in every exigency Mrs Radcliffe's heroines are provided with a pencil and paper, and the sun is never allowed to rise nor set in peace. . . in the most distressing circumstances [they] find time to compose sonnets to sunrise, the bat, a sea-nymph, a lily or a butterfly.'

Raine, Nigel (English scientist, twenty-first century). Bee expert Dr Raine averred, on the BBC *Today* programme in 2008, that 'there are differences in the ways serial killers and bees behave. Obviously.'

Rajneesh, Bhagwan Shree (Indian guru, 1931–90). While leading his cult of mysticism and free love, the Bhagwan accumulated a Lear jet, ninety-three Rolls-Royces, and thirty-five watches encrusted with precious gems. One of his henchwomen was charged with crimes including wiretapping, fire-bombing, poisoning, and the attempted murder of the Bhagwan's dentist. Bernard Levin described him as 'the conduit along which the vital force of the universe flows'.

Rand, Ayn (American writer, 1905–82). Ayn Rand was a passionate stamp collector. Her article 'Why I Like Stamp Collecting' appeared in the *Minkus Stamp Journal* in 1971. It is considerably shorter than her novel, *Atlas Shrugged*. At her funeral in 1982, 'It's A Long Way To Tipperary' was sung.

Rasputin, Maria (Russian writer, circus performer, riveter, and psychic, 1899–1977). In the United States during the 1930s, the daughter of Russian holy man Grigori Rasputin worked as a lion tamer and advertised breakfast cereal. 'To start the day right, I always recommend Wheaties.' she said.

Ray, Mary (English dog trainer, twenty-first century).

Interviewed at Crufts dog show in 2006, Mary Ray made the sensible observation that 'there's a big difference between dancing on your own and dancing with a dog'.

Reagan, Ronald (American actor and politician and POTUS, 1911–2004). When Reagan and his wife Nancy retired to California, friends bought a property for them at 666 St Cloud Road in Bel Air. Disturbed at their house number being the Number of the Beast, they persuaded the Bel Air authorities to change it to 668. Conspiracy theorists, however, were able to point to the fact that there were six letters each in the name 'Ronald Wilson Reagan', which was surely significant.

Reichenbach, Carl Ludwig Von (German scientist, 1788–1869). Von Reichenbach concocted the theory of Odic force, the Od being the vital energy in all living things. His book, *Physico-Physiological Researches on the Dynamics of Magnetism*, was praised by *Harper's New Monthly Magazine* in 1851. His investigations, it said, 'are of a singularly curious character, exhibiting the most astonishing developments, with a philosophical calmness that is rare even among German savants'.

Richard II (English king, 1367–1400). Neurotic King Richard is credited with the invention of the handker-chief. The record of his personal expenses includes a note specifying an order for cloths which must be 'little pieces made for giving to the lord King for carrying in his hand to wipe and cleanse his nose'.

Richet, Charles (French scientist and spiritualist, 1850–1935). Richet coined the word 'ectoplasm' after a séance in 1903. The luminous sticky white goo emitted by spiritualist mediums was also briefly known as 'teleplasm' and 'ideoplasm'.

Robert-Houdin, Jean Eugène (French magician, 1805–71). In *Recollections Of Robert-Houdin, Clockmaker, Electrician, Conjuror*, the magician remembered 'I not only investigated the so-called supernatural powers of the child known as the Infant Magnet, but, on a public stage, during the performance of certain mysterious phenomena by a young lady who shall be nameless, I consented to be locked up in a dark cabinet with that interesting maiden, whose *toilette* was superb.'

Robinson, Edward G., Junior (American actor and playboy, 1933–74). Growing up in Hollywood, the son of Edward G. Robinson spent so much time on the sets of his father's films that he developed a passion for prison cells. One of his birthday presents was a child-sized jail complete with bars and padlocks. By his early teens his behaviour was so wild that he often ended up in real police cells.

Ross, Harold (American journalist, 1892–1951). The founding editor of *The New Yorker* never read anything except submissions to the magazine. According to James Thurber, he owned only three books, one by Mark Twain, one by someone called Spencer whom he mistakenly thought was by Herbert Spencer, and the third a treatise on the migration of eels.

Rossetti, Dante Gabriel (English artist and poet, 1828–82). Benny Green gave a helpful summary of

Rossetti's life and career, to be imagined as a set of counters for a parlour game: 'the wombat, the Icelandic myths, the Fleshly School, the laudanum and the Stunners'.

Rousseau, Henri 'Douanier' (French painter, 1844–1910). When the elderly Rousseau went on trial in 1909 charged with fraud and embezzlement, his defence lawyer produced in court one of his 'jungle' paintings – all monkeys and oranges – as evidence that his client was obviously a simple soul incapable of committing calculated crimes. Rousseau was acquitted.

Ruby, Jack (American strip club owner, 1911–67). The favourite drink of the man who shot Lee Harvey Oswald (q.v.) was Doctor Brown's Celery Tonic, also known as Cel Ray, a celery-based decoction which came in a peculiarly-shaped bottle with expensive-looking gold foil wrapping. Ruby liked to give bottles of this, together with corned beef sandwiches, to Dallas cops and radio presenters.

Rumwold (English infant saint, b. 622). Saint Rumwold was born at King's Sutton in AD 622, the son of Saint Cyneburga and King Alchfrid. His first words, on the day he was born, were 'I am a Christian.' He then asked to be baptised, and to receive Holy Communion. The next day he preached a sermon, quoting freely from Scripture. On the third day he addressed another sermon, to his parents, and then he keeled over and died.

Ruskin, John (English writer, 1819–1900). As a child, Ruskin was not allowed any toys. His favourite pastime was digging holes in the garden, but he was not allowed to do that either. As a treat, on Sundays he was allowed to jump off his favourite box. He had a lifelong loathing of invalids, prompted initially by his cousin Margaret, who – apart from having a twisted spine – wore her hair in ringlets, which Ruskin could not bear the sight of.

Russell, Ken (English film director, 1927–2011). According to Glenda Jackson, the only direction Russell ever gave to his actors was to say, 'It needs to be a bit more . . . *urrrgh*', or 'a bit less *hmmm*'.

Ruth The Truth (English psychic agony aunt, b. 1968). It was due to her psychic powers that Ruth the Truth was able to tell 'Janet from Pembroke', in *Chat* magazine in March 2006, that the squirrel in Janet's garden had a message for her. The possibly earth-shattering contents of that message have never been divulged to the wider world.

Sadat, Anwar (Egyptian statesman and President, 1918–81). Sadat's favourite author was Barbara Cartland.

Saintsbury, George (English writer and critic, 1845–1933). Saintsbury was celebrated for the convolutions of his syntax, both written and spoken. One admirer transcribed a typical sentence: 'But while none, save these, of men living, had done, or could have done, such things, there was much here which – whether either could have done it or not – neither had done.'

Sand, Georges (French writer, real name Aurore Dupin Duvenant, 1804–76). Sand had a pet cricket named Cricri that lived in her writing desk, eating sealing wax and drinking ink. It was accidentally crushed by one of her servants.

Satie, Erik (French composer, 1866–1925). In the account of his daily routine given in *Memoirs Of An Amnesiac*, Satie claimed, 'My only nourishment consists of food that is white: eggs, sugar, shredded bones, the fat of dead animals, veal, salt, coconuts, chicken cooked in white water, mouldy fruit, rice, turnips, sausages in camphor, pastry, cheese (white varieties), cotton salad and certain kinds of fish (without their skin). I boil my wine and drink it cold mixed with the juice of the Fuchsia. I have a good appetite, but never talk when eating for fear of strangling myself.'

Sayn-Wittgenstein, Carolyne zu (Polish writer, 1819–87). After marriage to her lover Franz Liszt was forbidden, and he took holy orders, Sayn-Wittgenstein sank deeper and deeper into seclusion, and during the twenty-seven years she lived in Rome she left her home in the Via del Babuino only once, for twenty-four hours. She grew more and more immersed in the Church and its affairs. Gregorius said she fairly 'sputtered spirituality'. Her chief work during these years was a study, in twenty-four volumes, entitled *Interior Causes of the Exterior Weakness of the Church*, which she completed a few days before her death.

Scargill, Arthur (English trade unionist, b. 1938). Upon learning of the death of Margaret Thatcher in 2013, one of Scargill's friends sent him a text message stating 'Thatcher dead'. Moments later came the reply from the ageing revolutionary firebrand, in block capitals: 'SCARGILL LIVES!'

Schicklgruber, Alois (Austrian civil servant, 1837–1903). Like Sherlock Holmes, Adolf Hitler's father became increasingly obsessed with bee-keeping in later life.

Schieffelin, Eugene (American Bard and bird-lover,

1827–1906). Schieffelin was president of the American Acclimatization Society, and he had the bright idea of trying to introduce to the United States every type of bird mentioned in the works of Shakespeare. In 1890, Schieffelin released sixty common starlings in Central Park in New York. There are now estimated to be around 200 million starlings in the country.

Schleyer, Johann Martin (German priest, 1831–1912). During a sleepless night in 1879, Schleyer received a command from God telling him to create a universal language. As a result, he invented Volapük. Ten years later there were over two hundred Volapük clubs around the world and more than fifteen hundred accredited speakers. A striking feature of the language was the prevalence of umlauts. Schleyer explained 'A language without umlauts sounds monotonous, harsh, and boring.' Various followers, intimidated by the umlauts, created umlaut-free versions, including Nal Bino, Balta, Bopal, Spelin, Dil and Orba, but none of these caught on. The rise of Esperanto – which Schleyer dismissed as 'an ugly-sounding hodge-podge' – eventually eclipsed Volapük, though it is not entirely dead. An online Volapük Wikipedia provides thousands of articles and lessons for beginners.

Schmidt, Johannes (Danish biologist, 1877–1933). The man who discovered that eels spawn in the Sargasso Sea was also the author of the specialist tome, *Danish Eel Investigations During 25 Years, 1905–1930.*

Schubert, Franz (Austrian composer, 1797–1828). Upon his deathbed, Schubert's final wish was that someone would bring him some books by James Fenimore Cooper.

Scott, George R. (British poultry expert, twentieth century). Scott was the author of the 1934 book, *The Art Of Faking Exhibition Poultry*. In the introduction, Socrates, Galileo, Voltaire, Nietzsche and D. H. Lawrence are each called to support his attack on the despicable practice, nowhere more vile than in 'the pseudo-scientific Hogan cult, with all its blowsy jargon; its crapulous fundament of snide anatomy; its noisy and prolific drool of whim-wham'.

Scott, Sir Walter (Scottish novelist, 1771–1832). In Scott's 1826 novel *Woodstock, or The Cavalier*, a character named Tonkins meets a violent end. Scott regrets that 'his brains had not been beaten out in his cradle' to prevent him growing up into 'one of those Muggletonians'. For this insult he was on the receiving end of a formal Muggletonian curse, delivered by Robert Wallis, a Muggletonian from Islington. It is unknown if the curse was effective. *See* Muggleton, Lodowicke

Scriabin, Alexander (Russian composer, 1872–1915). For a pianist, Scriabin had surprisingly tiny hands. More than once he suffered sprains and injuries when relentlessly practising his own compositions. At the time of his death he left incomplete the *Mysterium*, a work involving an orchestra, dance, light, and exotic perfumes, to be performed in the Himalayas. Its playing would have ushered in Armageddon, the birth of a new world, and the emergence of a Nietzschean Superman.

Seward, Anna (English poet, 1742–1809). Anna Seward was Boswell's source for a story that the infant Samuel Johnson (q.v.) killed a duck by stamping on it. She was a poet, admired (in part) by Sir Walter Scott (q.v.), who after her death edited three volumes of her work, though he confessed that 'most of [it] is absolutely execrable'. In her letters she showed herself to be a titan of purple prose, rendering the sight of some rare woodcocks as 'the transmigratory gentry of dusky pinion are great strangers here', and, of the dying days of a friend, that 'the intellectual torch wavered not, neither dimmed in its earthly socket'.

Sheldon, May French (American explorer and writer, 1847–1936). Sheldon was of the view that if a man could go exploring in uncharted territories, then so too could a woman. Accordingly, in 1891 she set out, unaccompanied, for Africa, exploring the area around Lake Chala on the Kenya-Tanzania border. On her return, suffering from dysentery and with 'the doom of death upon me', she had to be carried in a palanquin. In her book, *Sultan To Sultan: Adventures among the Masai and other tribes of East Africa* (1892), she gave a characteristically dramatic account of a palanquin mishap. The party came to a bridge over a river swollen by rains: 'I should have walked across, however, without a thought of danger I allowed myself to be carried in my Palanquin; the bark proved to be unsound and slippery; my bearers maintained their footing with difficulty; when in the middle of the bridge, over the swollen torrent which noisily tumbled in its stony bed twenty or more feet below us, the bark peeled off from the logs, and the usually sure-footed porters were hurled with me down into the rushing waters, whereas they at their peril were dashed headlong into the dubious channel, and compelled to struggle for their lives. For a hazardous moment, only a moment, although time and space are so immeasurably elongated into eternities during like terrors, I was whirled about, protected from injury by my Palanquin, but with my head down and completely submerged in thick yellow water, in jeopardy of drowning. Several additional porters – for the bearers, poor fellows, had all they could do to save themselves – precipitously descended the bank and plunged into the seething waters and extricated me with great difficulty from the Palanquin in which I was helplessly buried beneath a confused mess of cushions, besides being underwater.'

Shelley, Percy Bysshe (English poet, 1792–1822). Sir John Rennie described Shelley as a boy: 'The least circumstance that thwarted him produced the most violent paroxysms of rage; and when irritated by other boys, he would take up anything or even any little boy near him, to throw at his tormentors. His imagination was always roving upon something romantic and extraordinary, such as spirits, fairies, fighting, volcanoes, etc., and he not unfrequently astonished his schoolfellows by blowing up the boundary palings of the playground with gunpowder.'

Sherwood, Henry Hall (Doctor and magnetism expert, nineteenth century). Sherwood was the inventor of the 'savage rotary magnetic machine' which he claimed could cure a variety of ailments including rheumatism, herpes, and tuberculosis. His theories made him briefly notorious in New York in the mid-nineteenth century, his contemporary Edward Giddins describing them as 'puerile in the extreme and full of absurdity'.

Shiel, M. P. (British writer, 1865–1947). Shiel was born on

Montserrat and later claimed to be Felipe I, King of Redonda, a tiny uninhabited rock a short distance north-west of the West Indian island. He named the poet John Gawsworth as both his literary executor and heir to the kingdom. Gawsworth kept Shiel's ashes in a biscuit tin on his mantelpiece. Rebecca West said that 'sensible people ought to have a complete set of Shiel'.

Shue, Zona Heaster (American murder victim and ghost, 1873?–97). Zona Shue was murdered by her ne'er-do-well husband Erasmus Stribbling Trout Shue in January 1897. The cause of death was initially certified as 'everlasting faint', but Zona's ghost manifested itself to her mother several times, explaining that her husband had killed her. He was eventually brought to trial and the evidence of Zona's ghost ruled admissible. Convicted on the basis of her testimony, Erasmus Shue died in prison in 1900.

Sibthorp, Charles de Laet Waldo (English politician, 1783–1855). 'Colonel' Sibthorp was a reactionary *par excellence*, who opposed all and any change in the order of things. He was particularly ferocious in his opposition to the railways, and to the Great Exhibition of 1851, which he deemed 'an exhibition of the trumpery and trash of foreigners who had no business to be here at all' and 'he offered a heartfelt prayer that Providence would think fit to destroy the impious project by a visitation of lightning'. He usually prefaced the word 'foreigners' with 'hypocritical', and offended Queen Victoria by so refer-ring to Prince Albert.

Simpson, Joe (English mountaineer, b. 1960). Simpson's book *Touching The Void* has become a modern classic, and is now taught as a set text in some schools. This has led to the author engaging with his young readers on Twitter. One youth there dismissed Simpson with the matchless phrase 'crevasse wanker'.

Sinclair, Iain (English writer, b. 1943). When Sinclair is at work at his writing desk, he is watched over by the baleful gaze of a half-size cardboard cut-out model of William S. Burroughs.

Sivulla, Jatkuu Seuraavalla (Finnish writer, non-existent). In 2005 Jatkuu Seuraavalla Sivulla was credited as the author of an article in the *Guardian*. The piece had been translated from Finnish, and 'jatkuu seuraavalla sivulla' means 'continued on the next page'.

Smart, Christopher (English poet, 1722–71). Between 1751 and 1753, the author of the demented masterpiece *Jubilate Agno* edited, and wrote most of, a magazine called *The Midwife*. Among his contributions was this recipe for bubble and squeak: 'Take of Beef, Mutton, or Lamb, or Veal, or any other meat, two Pounds and an half, or any other Quantity; let it lay in Salt, till the saline Particles have lock'd up all the Juices of the Animal, and render'd the Fibres too hard to be digested; then boil it over a Turf or Peat Fire, in a Brass Kettle cover'd with a Copper Lid, till it is much done. Then take Cabbage (that which is most windy, and capable of producing the greatest Report) and boil it in a Bell-Metal Pot till it is done enough, or if you think it proper, till it is done too much. Then slice the beef, and souse that and the Cabbage both in a Frying-Pan together, and let it bubble and squeak over a Charcoal Fire, for half an Hour, three Minutes, and two Seconds. Then eat a Quantum sufficit, or two Pounds and a half, and after it drink sixteen Pints of fat Ale, smoak, sleep, snoar, belch, and forget your Book.'

Smith, Albert (English writer and mountaineer, 1816–60). Smith was a well-known comic author by the time he climbed Mont Blanc in 1851, which led the *Daily News* to note that his ascent 'will be most appropriately recorded in a tissue of indifferent puns and stale fast witticisms with an incessant straining after smartness. The aimless scramble of the four pedestrians to the top of Mont Blanc will not go far to redeem the somewhat equivocal reputation of the herd of English tourists in Switzerland for a mindless and rather vulgar redundance of animal spirits'. Unabashed, Smith constructed a miniature model of the mountain and his show, *Mont Blanc In A Box*, was a Victorian hit, with at least two thousand performances in six years, including a private show at Osborne House for Queen Victoria and Prince Albert.

Smith, Dodie (English writer, 1896–1990). The author of *The Hundred And One Dalmatians* and *I Capture The Castle* had fond memories of her Auntie Bertha: 'She could not tell her right hand from her left unless she hopped, and she insisted that if she was left alone for more than three hours her teeth went soft.' She always added the words 'Burn this' at the end of every letter she wrote.

Smith, George Albert (English hypnotist, psychic, and film pioneer, 1864–1959). Smith has been hailed as the father of British cinema for his pioneering technical innovations. Before turning to film, he was a stage hypnotist and leading member of the Society for Psychical Research. Trevor H. Hall wrote of him in 1964: 'Most of the early work of the Society on thought-transference ... relied entirely upon the integrity of Smith and the assumed reality of his unusual gifts. His large circle of youthful and mainly uneducated male acquaintances in Brighton, used as paid hypnotic subjects by the founders of the S.P.R., has been the subject of speculative gossip for forty years.'

Smythe, F. S. (English mountaineer, 1900–49). Smythe took part in the International Kanchenjunga Expedition of 1930, during which he noted the first stirrings of 'Hitlerism' among his German companions. Every member of the expedition 'was issued with a flag which he was expected to keep flying over his tent. It was the ambition of the Germans to plant their flags on the top of each mountain. The emblem issued to me was a Union Jack with the stripes the wrong way round, made in Germany. Running short of pocket handkerchiefs on one occasion I used it as a substitute to the horror of my German companions. Possibly, indeed, the alleged decay of democracy dates from this.'

Southey, Robert (English poet, 1774–1843). In 1821, Southey invited William Wordsworth and his wife to dinner and served them roast owl. Wordsworth was 'not valiant' enough to eat it, though Mrs Wordsworth tucked in. Southey later admitted that the owl should have been 'boiled and smothered in onions'.

Spears, Britney (American popstrel, b. 1981). It was said, unkindly, of Mr and Mrs Spears that they meant to give their daughter the (unaccountably popular) name

Brittany, but did not know how to spell it. In fact they dubbed her Britney so that her full name would be an anagram of Presbyterians.

Speedwell, Germander (English wordsmith, twenty-first century). Speedwell's *Sayings* include 'Nothing is interesting unless it can be catalogued.'

Speke, John Hanning (English explorer, 1827–64). One night when Speke was searching for the source of the Nile, his tent became infested with small black beetles. He was awakened by one of them crawling into his ear, where it 'began with exceeding vigour, like a rabbit in a hole, to dig violently away at my tympanum. The queer sensation this amusing measure excited in me is past description'. Speke tried and failed to flush the beetle out with melted butter, then dug into his ear with his penknife. He killed but did not manage to remove the insect, and the resulting infection twisted his face, caused boils, made him almost deaf, and ate a hole between his ear and his nose. When he blew his nose, 'my ear whistled so audibly that those who heard it laughed'.

Spencer, Diana (English princess, 1961–97). Princess Diana cheerfully admitted to being 'as thick as a plank'. Her finest academic achievement was to win a school prize for best-kept guinea pig.

Spencer, Herbert (English philosopher, 1820–1903). Spencer had a suit specially made for him which he only wore when he was feeling irritable. Sometimes he wore it for weeks at a time. It was made of one piece, of soft soothing material, and had an intricate system of lacing at the front. His family called it 'the angry suit'.

Spencer-Stanhope, Anna Maria Wilhelmina (English aristocrat, 1824–1901). Lady Spencer-Stanhope advertised for a butler. She interviewed an applicant, a neat, respectable, and well-spoken man, who explained that he was currently employed as a valet to the head of a lunatic asylum but could no longer bear to be surrounded by people 'not in their right minds'. The interview was going well until the man spotted silverware on the table and became transfixed, his eyes staring wildly. When he reached out to grasp a knife, Lady Spencer-Stanhope made an excuse to end the discussion and had him shown out. She later received a letter from the doctor at the asylum. 'The man you ask me about is very intelligent and well-educated, and formerly bore an excellent character. But unfortunately he was not a valet here, as he imagines, but a patient. He is a homicidal maniac and some years ago committed a peculiarly brutal murder. He is now, strongly against my advice, allowed out on probation, but I consider it most dangerous as I feel certain that sooner or later he will have a recurrence of the homicidal mania.'

Spinoza, Baruch (Dutch philosopher, 1632–77). To relax after protracted periods of study, Spinoza liked to set two spiders to fight each other. As he watched their combats, he would be seized with fits of immoderate laughter.

Stanhope, Lady Hester (English traveller, 1776–1839). Lady Hester Stanhope read a prophecy which stated: 'A European female would come to live on Mount Lebanon, and build a house there and obtain power and influence greater than the Sultan; that the coming of the Mahdi, the great prophet, would follow, but would be preceded by war, pestilence, famine and other calamities, that the Mahdi would ride a horse born saddled and that a woman would come from a far country to take part in his mission and triumph.' Assuming that the Mahdi in fact meant the Messiah, and that she would become his bride, she travelled to the Lebanon, moved into a monastery, and struck fear into the local inhabitants and into the tyrannical Prince of the Druzes, who was petrified of her. She boasted that she could administer a slap in the face more effectively than anyone else in the world. Alas, neither Mahdi nor Messiah turned up, and she died a penniless recluse.

Starr, Ringo (English children's television entertainer, real name Richard Starkey, b. 1940). In a *Daily Telegraph* photo-spread of celebrities attending the 2010 Chelsea Flower Show, a caption identified Starr (correctly) as 'the narrator of *Thomas The Tank Engine*', a popular children's television show. Readers were not told that in his twenties Starr was the drummer in a pop group called The Beatles.

Stein, Gertrude (American writer, 1874–1946). Stein liked to write while looking at cows. She and Alice B. Toklas would drive around until they found a suitable spot, then Stein would sit on a campstool armed with pad and pencil, while Toklas coaxed a cow into her line of vision. *See* Ure, Midge

Stendhal (French writer, real name Marie-Henri Beyle, 1783–1842). Stendhal believed that an efficacious cure for the pangs of love was to eat lots of peas.

Stephen, Leslie (English writer, 1832–1904). As a child, Virginia Woolf's father was diagnosed by a doctor as having 'disordered circulation'. The cure prescribed was 'fresh air, humdrum lessons, and a rigorous abstinence from poetry', so his mother sent him to Eton. Later in life, Stephen enjoyed organising lengthy hikes known as 'Sunday Tramps', usually covering about fifty miles. He was also a keen mountaineer, and wrote a number of essays on the subject including 'A Bad Five Minutes In The Alps'.

Sterne, Laurence (Anglo-Irish writer, 1713–68). Shortly after being buried in St George's churchyard in Hanover Square, Sterne's corpse was stolen by resurrectionists who delivered it to anatomists at Cambridge University. One among their number, however, had been a friend of Sterne's, recognised him, and arranged for the cadaver to be returned – discreetly – for reburial.

Stevens, Wallace (American poet, 1879–1955). Like Charles Ives (q.v.) and Franz Kafka (q.v.), Wallace Stevens held down a full-time job in the insurance industry while pursuing a parallel creative career. In 1936, the cerebral poet was involved in one of the great – if brief – literary spats of the decade when he was engaged in a fist-fight with Ernest Hemingway. At a party, Hemingway's sister reported tearfully to her brother that (not for the first time) Stevens was describing him as 'a sap'. Novelist and poet faced up to each other in the street outside. Stevens broke his hand socking Hemingway on the jaw. Hemingway knocked Stevens into a puddle, and later wrote: 'I think he is really one of those mirror fighters who swells his muscles and practices lethal punches in the bathroom while he hates his betters.'

Stevenson, Robert Louis (Scottish writer, 1850–94). Stevenson died while making mayonnaise. His wife found him collapsed, from a probable cerebral haemorrhage, on the kitchen floor of their home in Samoa.

Stokes, Doris (English spiritualist medium, 1920–87). Doris Stokes was born in Grantham, Lincolnshire, and grew up one street away from the young Margaret Thatcher. It is amusing to posit an alternative history where each followed the other's career path. Doris Stokes briefly became disenchanted with spiritualism in the early 1960s and retrained, appropriately, as a psychiatric nurse. She abandoned the profession after being attacked by a patient.

Struther, Jan (English writer, real name Joyce Anstruther, 1901–53). The creator of wartime housewife heroine Mrs Miniver once had a terrible road journey in France, during which the car became stuck in mud in bad visibility, she was shouted at by an angry farmer while stuck behind pigs, obstructed by a fallen tree athwart the road, and one of the tyres suffered a puncture. 'Our delay was due to bog, fog, frog, hog and log, and if only I could make out that the puncture was due to a loose cog, my happiness would be complete' she wrote.

Stuart, Henry Frederick (Scottish, Prince of Wales, 1594–1612). When King James I's son was welcomed into the

Merchant Taylors' Company in 1601, they laid on a feast for him: 'Swans, godwit, shovellers, partridges, owls, cuckoos, ringdoves, pullets, ducklings, teal, peacocks, rabbits, leverets and a great turkey... along with 1,300 eggs, three great lobsters and 200 prawns, salmon, salt fish, plaice, sole, dory, carp and tenches, sirloins and ribs of beef, mutton and lambs' dowsets, neats' tongues and sweet breads, and to conclude the evening, figs, dates, prunes, currants, almonds, strawberries, gooseberries, cherries, pears, apples, damsons, oranges and quinces. Twenty-eight barrels of beer were provided to slake the diners' thirst, together with more than 440 gallons of wine.'

Swedenborg, Emanuel (Swedish mystic, 1688–1772). Around the age of thirty, Swedenborg was deeply in love with one Emerentia Polhem. When she turned down his offer of marriage, he was flung into despair, which he coped with by devoting himself to the study of tin plate, a subject on which he then published a pamphlet. Some years later, in London, Swedenborg stripped off his clothing, threw his money to the mob, and leapt into a muddy ditch at Cold Bath Fields, rolling around in the filth. This episode followed certain shamanic visions and ravings. The Swedenborg Society, based in Bloomsbury in London, was founded in 1810 and continues to flourish.

Swinburne, Algernon Charles (English poet, 1837–1909). In the bloom of youth, Swinburne would attend parties with a sheaf of manuscripts stuffed inside his jacket. Awaiting an opportunity to drop into the conversation the fact that he happened to have a poem or two upon his person, he counted on someone to insist that he must read it to the assembled company. He would then oblige, accompanying the rhythms of his verse with strange little skips and jumps, startling and embarrassing his listeners. As he got more and more carried away by his own delivery, Swinburne's voice would rise to a shrill, high-pitched scream.

Sylvester, Joshua (English poet, 1563–1618). Sylvester's works were dismissed by John Dryden as 'abominable fustian'. In 1615 he published an anti-smoking broadside entitled *Tobacco Battered and the Pipes Shattered about their Eares, that idely Idolize so base and barbarous a Weed, or at least overlove so loathsome a Vanity, by a Volley of Holy Shot Thundered from Mount Helicon.*

Symmes, John Cleves (American hollow earth theorist, 1779–1829). Symmes announced his theory on 10 April 1818 in *Circular No. 1*:

TO ALL THE WORLD: I declare that the earth is hollow and habitable within; containing a number of solid concentric spheres, one within the other, and that it is open at the poles twelve or sixteen degrees. I pledge my life in support of this truth, and am ready to explore the hollow, if the world will support and aid me in this undertaking. N. B. I have ready for the press a Treatise on the Principles of the matter, wherein I show proofs of the above position, account for the various phenomena, and disclose Dr. Darwin's 'Golden Secret'. I ask one hundred brave companions, well equipped, to start from Siberia in the fall season, with reindeer and sleighs, on the ice of the frozen sea; and I engage we find a warm and rich land, stocked with thrifty vegetables and animals, if not men, on reaching one degree northwest of latitude 62°; we will return in the succeeding spring.

There were to be many more *Circulars*, and many supporters, not least Edgar Allan Poe (q.v.), but almost two hundred years later 'Symmes' Hole', portal to the underworld, remains undiscovered.

Taylor, Elizabeth (English actress, 1932–2011). Upon the release of *This Is It*, a film composed primarily of cobbled-together rehearsal footage for the shows Michael Jackson was preparing at the time of his death, Elizabeth Taylor pronounced it 'the single most brilliant piece of film-making I have ever seen'.

Taylor, Harriet (English philosopher, 1807–58). Harriet Taylor received a letter from her husband John Stuart Mill, perplexed at her ability to break the habit of spitting. 'When you cough are you not obliged to swallow something if you do not spit it up?' he asked. Her reply suggested it was simply a matter of willpower. 'I cannot but think,' she wrote, 'that if you tried as earnestly as I have done since October to avoid any expectoration that you would lose the habit altogether as I have done.'

Taylor, Joseph (English writer, 1761 or 1762–1844). Taylor was the author of *Apparitions or, The Mystery of Ghosts, Hobgoblins, and Haunted Houses Developed. Being A Collection Of Entertaining Stories, Founded On Fact, And Selected For The Purpose Of Eradicating Those Fears, Which The Ignorant, The Weak, And The Superstitious, Are But Too Apt To Encourage, For Want Of Properly Examining Into The Causes Of Such Absurd Impositions* (1815), wherein he observed, *inter alia*, that 'idiots in general are remarkably fond of any thing relative to a funeral procession'.

Tebbit, Norman (English politician, b. 1931). In 2010, Tebbit prompted the glorious headline 'Norman Tebbit attacks child in dragon outfit'. The story below explained, somewhat disappointingly, that he 'was so upset by the noise caused by a Chinese New Year celebration near his home that he ran 100 yards down the street, grabbed a drum that someone was banging, and planted a kick on the backside of a dancing dragon – without realising a boy was inside'.

Teed, Cyrus Reed (American messiah, 1839–1908). Teed devised Koreshanity, which taught that the earth is hollow and that we live on the inner surface. Outside the sphere there is nothing. It was more than merely a scientific theory, however. Teed explained 'to know of the earth's concavity is to know God, while to believe in the earth's convexity is to deny Him and all His works. All that is opposed to Koreshanity is antichrist.' He founded a colony of believers in Florida, planning for eight million to be accommodated though only two hundred turned up. The colony survived until 1961.

Teilo (British saint, *c.* 500–*c.* 560). So well-loved and venerated was Saint Teilo, the Bishop of Pembrokeshire, that when he died three different churches in the area fought over which should claim his remains. His corpse miraculously split into three identical bodies, each of which is the 'real' Teilo, and they are buried at Llandaff Cathedral, Llandeilo Fawr, and Penally Abbey.

Thatcher, Margaret (English politician and Prime

Minister, 1925–2013). One of the great controversies provoked by Margaret Thatcher was the question of which bird she most closely resembled when in motion. Commentators were unable to agree. Matthew Parris of *The Times* claimed she walked like a partridge, while Jon Snow of *Channel 4 News* asserted that she scuttled about like a hen.

Theophrastus (Greek philosopher, *c.* 371–*c.* 287 BC). Theophrastus was a man with a wide range of interests. He wrote 'Three Books of the Gods; one of Enthusiasm; an Epitome of Natural Things; A tract against Naturallists; one Book of Nature; three more of Nature; two Abridgments of natural things; eighteen more of Natural things; seventeen of various Opinions concerning Natural things; one of Natural Problems; three of Motions; two more of Motion; three of Water; one of a River in Sicily; two of Meteors; two of Fire; one of Heaven; one of Nitre and Alum; two of things that putrifie; one of Stones; one of Metals; one of things that melt and coagulate; one of the Sea; one of Winds; two of things in dry places; two of Sublime things; one of Hot and Cold; one of Generation; ten of the History of Plants; eight of the causes of them; five of Humours; one of Melancholy; one of Honey; eighteen first Propositions concerning Wine; one of Drunkenness; one of Spirits; one of Hair; another of Juices, Flesh and Leather; one of things the sight of which is unexpected; one of things which are subject to wounds and bitings; seven of Animals, and another six of Animals; one of Man; one of Animals that are thought to participate of Reason; One of the Prudence and Manners, or Inclinations of Animals; one of Animals that dig themselves Holes and Dens; one of fortuitous

Animals; 1182 Verses comprehending all sorts of Fruits and Animals; A question concerning the Soul; one of Sleeping and Waking; one of Labours; one of old Age; one of Thoughts; four of the Sight; one of things that change their Colour; one of Tears entituled *Callisthenes*; two of hearing; one of the Diversity of Voices of Animals of the same sort; one of Odours; two of Torment; one of Folly; one of the Palsie; one of the Epilepsie; one of the vertigo, and dazling of the Sight; one of the fainting of the Heart; one of Suffocation; one of Sweat; one of the Pestilence'.

Theseus (Founder-king of Athens). Theseus not only founded the city of Athens, he also, according to John Ruskin, invented mixed vegetable soup.

Thornton, Alice (English memoirist, 1626–1707). Alice Thornton's wedding day was dramatic. 'A deliverance from death that day I was married Dec. 15th, 1651,' she wrote. 'That very day on which I was married having been in good health and strength for many years before, I fell so suddenly ill and sick after one o'clock in the afternoon, that I thought, and all that saw me did believe it would have been my last night, being surprised with a violent pain in the head and stomach, causing great vomiting and sickness at my heart which lasted eight hours before I had any intermission: but blessed be the Lord our God, the Father of Mercies, which had compassion on me. I was pretty well about ten at night.' The mystery of what had befallen her did not last long, for Alice recalled that the night before she had sat up late and washed her feet, 'which is very dangerous at this time of year'.

Tippett, Michael (English composer, 1905–98). Tippett called the refrigerator in his kitchen 'Bernard Levin'.

Titivillus (Patron demon of scribes). Titivillus was an evil spirit in medieval legend who carried off to hell the words in church services which priests skipped over or mutilated. These literary scraps he deposited in a pit paved with good intentions that had never been fulfilled.

Tollemache-Tollemache, Ralph William Lyonel (English clergyman, 1826–95). Tollemache-Tollemache (originally Tollemache; he added the second Tollemache and became double-barrelled at the age of fifty) fathered ten children with his second wife Dora Cleopatra Maria Lorenza de Orellana, the daughter of an officer in the Spanish army. They had fun at the font, naming the children as follows:

Dora Viola G.I. de Orellana Plantagenet.

Mabel Helmingham Ethel Huntingtower Beatrice Blazonberrie Evangeline Vise de Lou de Orellana Plantagenet Toedmag Saxon.

Lyonesse Matilda Dora Ida Agnes Ernestine Curson Paulet Wilbraham Joyce Eugenie Bentley Saxonia Dysart Plantagenet.

Lyulph Ydwallo Odin Nestor Egbert Lyonel Toedmag Hugh Erchenwyne Saxon Esa Cromwell Orma Nevill Dysart Plantagenet.

Lyona Decima Veroica Esyth Undine Cyssa Hylda Rowena Adela Thyra Ursuala Ysabel Blanche Lelias Dysart Plantagenet.

Leo Quintus Tollemache-Tollemache de Orellana Plantagenet.

Lyonella Fredegunda Cuthberga Ethelswytha Ideth Ysabel Grace Monica de Orellana Plantagenet.

Leone Sextus Denys Oswolf Fraudifilius Tollemache-Tollemache de Orellana Plantagenet.

Lyonetta Edith Regina Valentine Myra Polwarth Avelina Phillipa Violantha de Orellana Plantagenet.

Lyunulph Cospatrick Bruce Berkeley Jermyn Tullibardine Petersham de Orellana Dysart Plantagenet.

Topsell, Edward (English writer and cleric, *c.* 1572–1625). Topsell was the author of a bestiary entitled *The History Of Four-footed Beasts And Serpents: Describing at Large Their True and Lively Figure, their Several Natures, Conditions, Kinds, Virtues (both Natural and Medicinal) Countries of their Breed, their Love and Hatred to Mankind, and the wonderful work of God in their Creation, Perfection, and Destruction, Interwoven with curious variety of Historical Narrations out of Scriptures, Papers, Philosophers, Physicians and Poets.* Among the animals included was the Mimick, a type of dog conceived of an ape, which was able to 'imitate all things it seeth'. Plutarch reportedly saw a Mimick take part in a drama, presented before the Roman Emperor, in which the beast played several parts including a death scene in which it 'began to reel and stagger to and fro like a drunken man'.

Townson, Robert (English bishop, 1575–1621). Townson, who attended Sir Walter Raleigh at his execution, had a pet frog called Musidora which he kept to guard his dessert from flies.

Trollope, Anthony (English writer, 1815–82). Trollope's reputation as a bad-tempered, bullying, semi-unhinged maniac was such that at his first meeting with his publishers Chapman & Hall, Edward Chapman kept a firm grasp on a poker throughout the interview as a precaution. Trollope's demeanour may in part have been caused by the fact that throughout his life he was haunted by the unjust accusation – made when he was a pupil at Sunbury School – that he had engaged in 'some nameless horror' with four other boys.

Trotsky, Leon (Russian revolutionary, 1879–1940). Trotsky first met Stalin in a house on Whitechapel Road in the East End of London. On the site today is a McDonald's restaurant.

Tupper, Martin Farquhar (English writer, 1810–89). The best-selling Victorian author had a dreadful stutter that prevented him being able to follow his chosen career as a preacher. In one attempt to cure it, he undertook a daily drill of reading aloud, for hours at a time, in deliberately monotonous tones, syllable by syllable and with a crutch under his tongue, Milton's *Paradise Lost*. When he had read that in its entirety he embarked upon the complete poems of Cowper. He was prescribed emulcents and styptics, without success. He eventually took a job as a scrivener, where he would not need to speak, and then wrote his *Proverbial Philosophy,* one of the most popular books of the nineteenth century.

Tyson, Mike (American boxer, b. 1966). As a child, Tyson developed a great love of birds, particularly pigeons. One day, when a neighbourhood tough ripped the head off a pigeon, Tyson was so upset he attacked the older boy. Thus he discovered his ferocious fighting skills and resolved to become a boxer.

Ure, Midge (Scottish musician, b. 1953). In homage to Midge Ure's beat combo, the Kansas cattle rancher Kirk Dickinson named one of his cows Ultravox. *See* Williams, Margo

Van Dyke, Dick (American actor, b. 1925). It is an unforgettable headline: 'Porpoises Rescue Dick Van Dyke'. The story, reported in the *Guardian* in 2010, told how the octogenarian chimney sweep dozed off on his surfboard in the Pacific Ocean and woke to find himself adrift and out of sight of land. He feared death, until a pod of 'friendly porpoises' appeared and pushed him ashore. Three years later, another newspaper headline informed us 'Dick Van Dyke Rescued From Burning Car'. No porpoises seem to have been involved in the latter incident, more's the pity.

Van Vliet, Don (American musician, aka Captain Beefheart, 1941–2010). There is an oft-repeated though possibly apocryphal story that when, as a young man in California, Van Vliet was working as a door-to-door vacuum cleaner salesman, he knocked one day at the door of the desert-dwelling English writer Aldous Huxley. Van Vliet's sales pitch was to announce: 'I assure you, sir, this thing sucks,' whereupon Huxley duly purchased one.

Vaughan, Mr (English Ranter, seventeenth century). Vaughan was the target of an anonymous pamphlet of 1650 entitled *Hell broke loose: or, the notorious design of the wicked Ranters, discovered on Sunday last at Black-Fryers Being a true relation of the strange proceedings of Mr. Vaughan, and*

his wicked proselytes; and their entring of Black-Fryers church in
sermon time, like so many spirits from hell, with four damnable
papers in the hands, containing such horrible, audacious, and
abominable songs, the like not to be parallel'd in former ages.
With the manner how this insolent Ranter traced the streets from
Black-Fryers to Saint Paul's Church-yard, in his Holland shirt,
without doublet or breeches, a treble cap, like the Pope's miter,
with silk fring, and white shooes, and stockings. With their
damnable plots, and conspiracies against the ministers of the
gospel: their examination before the right honourable the Lord
Mayor of London; the sad and woful speeches, made by the
ringleader of the Ranters, concerning the city magistrates, and
golden chains: and the committing of them to Bridewell till the
next sessions.

Ventham, Wanda (English actress, b. 1935). Ventham, the
mother of actor Benedict Cumberbatch, has an extensive
collection of stuffed barn owls.

VerEecke, Robert (American Jesuit, dancer and choreog-
rapher, b. 1948). One of Father VerEecke's most overwhelming creations was splendidly described by critic
Wilma Salisbury: 'As an introduction to the Jesuit priest's
choreography, Kahn performed *Overwhelmed*, an expres-
sionistic evocation of a dark emotional state that
suggested sacred dance only in a few gestures of prayer.
Set to a recording of prepared piano music by John Cage,
the brief piece ended with the exhausted dancer lying in
a heap as the stage darkened. When the lights came up,
Kahn had disappeared, and VerEecke had taken her
place in the same crumpled position. Rising from the
floor, he cried out to God, ran around the periphery of
the stage and pounded his fists against the rear wall. His

185

cries of the heart were picked up and developed in lyrical movements by ten dancers who had learned the graceful choreography in VerEecke's workshop.'

Verne, Jules (French writer, 1828–1905). The pioneer of science fiction had fractious relationships with the younger generation of Vernes. He persuaded a magistrate to imprison his teenage son Michel, not for any specific offence, but merely to teach him a lesson. Some years later, his nephew Gaston, having escaped from a lunatic asylum, lay in wait for Verne outside his house and, when the writer arrived home, fired two pistol shots, badly injuring him in the foot.

Vespasian (Roman emperor, 9–79). As he lay dying, Vespasian's last words were *'Væ, puto deus fio'*, that is 'Oh! I am becoming a god'.

Victoria (English queen, 1819–1901). When Albert, the Prince Consort, died in 1861, among the condolences Victoria received was a letter from a clergyman telling her that 'henceforth Christ himself will be your husband'. The Queen commented to a friend, 'That is what I call twaddle.'

Vidocq, Eugène François (French criminal and detective, 1775–1857). In the earlier, criminal, part of his career, Vidocq was so skilled at escaping from the clutches of the police that he was thought to have supernatural powers. One officer reported that he was a werewolf, while another testified that, at the moment he placed his hands on Vidocq to arrest him, the master criminal transformed himself into a bale of straw.

Vignoli, Tito (Italian philosopher, 1829–1914). Vignoli wrote about the power of daydreams, and our ability to 'see' images in a waking state that are the figments of our imagination. Belief in the reality of such images, he said, was 'particularly common in the lower classes'.

Vinegar Tom (English witch, seventeenth century). Vinegar Tom was one of the witches discovered by Matthew Hopkins. In *The Discovery Of Witches* (1647), Hopkins described him as looking like a greyhound with the head of an ox, with a long tail and broad eyes. Confronted by the Witchfinder General, however, he was transformed into the likeness of 'a child of foure yeeres old without a head'. He did half a dozen turns about the house and vanished at the door. *See* Wesley, Samuel

Voliva, Wilbur Glenn (American evangelist, 1870–1942). Voliva propounded the Flat Earth theory, part of his reasoning being that if we lived on a spinning globe, then if you jumped up in the air, you would come to land some distance away. His ideas about the sun were not dissimilar to those of Lodowicke Muggleton (q.v.). 'The idea of a sun millions of miles in diameter and 91,000,000 miles away is silly,' he wrote. 'The sun is only 32 miles across and not more than 3,000 miles from the earth. It stands to reason it must be so. God made the sun to light the earth, and therefore must have placed it close to the task it was designed to do. What would you think of a man who built a house in Zion and put the lamp to light it in Kenosha, Wisconsin?' Voliva was the first American evangelist to have his own radio station. He predicted that the world would end in 1923. Then in 1927. Then in 1930. Then again in 1935.

Wallace, William Herbert (English insurance agent and acquitted murder suspect, 1878–1933). Wallace was convicted of the mysterious murder of his wife Julia, but acquitted on appeal. The events took place in Liverpool in 1931. One of the key locations was Menlove Avenue, the road where Beatle John Lennon grew up. The evening before the murder, Wallace played chess with a man named McCartney, and on the day of the killing itself, he paid a visit to a Mrs Harrison. Alas, there is no record of the involvement of anyone called Starr or Starkey.

Walpole, Horace (English writer, 1717–97). In his voluminous writings, especially in his letters, Walpole was a great coiner of words, his most successful invention being *serendipity*. He also devised *nincompoophood* and other words deserving of revival. When the future King George III was a teenager, his grandfather tried to marry him off to a European princess, much to the dismay of George's mother. The name of the princess was Sophia Caroline Maria, daughter of the Duchess of Brunswick-Wolfenbüttel. Under his mother's influence, George became fretful and aghast at the proposal, and – as Walpole wrote – he 'declares violently against being *bewolfenbuttled* – a word I do not pretend to understand as it is not in Mr Johnson's new dictionary'. It should have been.

Warhol, Andy (American artist, 1928–87). Warhol was an extremely devout Roman Catholic who went to Mass daily. He often spent evenings doing voluntary work at a shelter for homeless people organised by the Church of the Heavenly Rest on the corner of Fifth Avenue and Ninetieth Street in Manhattan.

Warlock, Peter (English composer, real name Philip Heseltine, 1894–1930). Warlock was declared unfit for military service during the First World War on account of general neurasthenia and 'an inability to micturate when mentally excited, and especially in the presence of other people, with the consequence that he has had occasional prolonged retention,' according to a Harley Street doctor's report. As a seemingly fit young man swanning about London, he was subjected to insults from 'officious patriots'. His common retort was to declaim, loudly, these lines from Samuel Butler's *Psalm Of Montreal*:

O brother-in-law to Mr. Spurgeon's haberdasher,
Who seasonest also the skins of Canadian owls,
Thou callest trousers 'pants', whereas I call them
    'trousers',
Therefore thou art in hell-fire, and may the Lord pity
    thee!

Warner, Jack (English actor, 1895–1981). Invited to contribute a recipe to *A Kitchen Goes To War*, a 1940 government-issued cookbook, the man who later played the lead role in *Dixon of Dock Green* excelled himself with

'Cheese And Chutney Biscuits'. This consists of water biscuits, spread with margarine, topped with slices of cheese. Plus chutney.

Waters, Roger (English musician, b. 1943). Aged eighteen, Waters was imprisoned and kept in irons for more than a year. Oh, dammit! Unfortunately, this was not the Pink Floyd person, but a sixteenth-century Separatist Puritan of the same name.

Watts, George Frederic (English painter, 1817–1904). Watts hated his surname, and was jealous of his friend Tennyson for having three syllables. Late in life, after refusing a baronetcy, he wrote in his diary: 'The honour I should like would be that the Queen would invest me with a name pleasant to my ears and that would be a constant incentive, such as Tryamain or Fainhope; does this seem very silly?'

Waugh, Auberon (English writer, 1939–2001). While stationed in Cyprus during his National Service, Waugh noted that the machine gun mounted on his armoured car seemed to be faulty. When the convoy made a brief halt, he took the opportunity to dismount, seize the barrel of the gun from the front, and give it 'a good wiggle'. It then started firing, and he was shot six times in the shoulder, chest, and arm. He described the experience as 'almost completely painless'.

Wells, H. G. (English writer, 1866–1946). Wells was bothered by shaving, washing, answering letters, talking to people, doing up parcels and finding pieces of string or envelopes or stamps. One of his lesser-known works is his 1933 novel *The Bulpington Of Blup*, subtitled *Adventures, Poses, Stresses, Conflict, and Disaster in a Contemporary Brain.*

Weschke, Karl (German artist, 1925–2005). Weschke was by turns a member of the Luftwaffe, a Peak Freans' biscuit factory worker and an assistant lion tamer before settling in Cornwall to concentrate on painting. Asked if he had chosen to live there because of the quality of the light, he snorted, 'Cornish light? I've got a 60-watt light-bulb and I keep the curtains closed.'

Wesley, Samuel (English clergyman and poet, 1662–1735). On Christmas Day 1716, Wesley was haunted by an apparition of a badger with no head. It was called Jeffrey.

West, Mae (American actress and writer, 1893–1980). The inspiration for Mae West's famous line 'Beulah, peel me a grape' in *I'm No Angel* (1933) came from Boogie, her pet monkey. Boogie, she said, was a very fastidious monkey, who 'never ate a grape without peeling it first – and he ate a lot of grapes'.

Whicker, Alan (English journalist and broadcaster, 1921–2013). In a 1964 BBC documentary entitled *Death In The Morning*, Whicker observed that 'in Britain, any book about a gull or a duck, no matter how stumbling or inane, is an automatic bestseller'.

Whistler, James Abbott McNeill (American painter, 1834–1903). Invited to a country house shooting party, Whistler missed the grouse he was aiming at and accidentally shot his host's dog. 'It was a dog without artistic habits,' he said, 'and had placed itself badly in relation to the landscape.'

Wilde, Oscar Fingal O'Flahertie Wills (Irish writer, 1854–1900). Wilde's *The Picture Of Dorian Gray* was received with disfavour by some contemporary critics. The *Scots Observer* complained that he was writing for 'outlawed noblemen and perverted telegraph boys'. The *Daily Chronicle* called it 'a poisonous book, the atmosphere of which is heavy with mephitic odours of moral and spiritual putrefaction' and for The *Athenaeum* it was 'unmanly, sickening, vicious and tedious'. 'Paterfamilias' in *Uplift*, meanwhile, declared, 'I would rather give my daughter a dose of prussic acid than allow her to read this book.'

Wildman, Daniel (English bee enthusiast, eighteenth century). In June 1772, a newspaper announcement appeared: 'Exhibition of bees on horseback! At the Jubilee Gardens, Islington, this and every evening until further notice (wet evenings excepted). The celebrated Daniel Wildman will exhibit several new and amazing experiments, never attempted by any man in this or any other kingdom before. He rides standing upright, one foot on the saddle and one on the neck, with a mask of bees on his head and face. He also rides standing upright on the saddle with the bridle in his mouth, and, by firing a pistol makes one part of the bees march over the table, and the other swarm in the air and return to their hive again, with other performances too tedious to insert.'

Willcox, Toyah (English popstrel, b. 1958). Mindful of her status as a cultural icon, Toyah Willcox maintains a property solely for the storage of her archive, including press cuttings, costumes, stage make-up, fan mail, and VHS recordings of all her appearances on *Top Of The Pops*.

William I (English-Norman king, *c.* 1028–87). At the coronation of William the Conqueror in Westminster Abbey on Christmas Day 1066, some of the Norman knights present were so alarmed by the ceremonial *collaudatio*, or great roar of acclamation, that they burned down many of the buildings surrounding the Abbey.

William IV (British king, 1765–1837). Edith Sitwell described William IV as 'that very excitable, choleric, good-natured old gentleman, with his popping, bobbling gestures, his habit of exploding into a room rather than entering it, his obstinacy allied so strangely with extreme changeableness, his ideas that floated in and out of his mind as if they were blown by a sea-gale, his head shaped like a pineapple, and his eyes that floated on the surface of his face as if they were bubbles. Mr Greville remarked that "King William had considerable facility in expressing himself, but what he said was generally useless and improper."'

Williams, Kenneth (English actor, 1926–88). Williams never allowed anyone into the pristine central London flat he shared with his mother. 'I can't stand the idea of another bottom on my loo,' he explained.

Williams, Margo (English psychic, twentieth century). Margo Williams used her psychic gifts to find objects on the Isle of Wight. Apprised of a location by one of her spirit guides, and having no transport of her own, she called on one of her team of helpers to drive her to the spot. The helper would bring a spade or shovel to do the usually necessary digging work, and wear old clothes, for Isle of Wight ghosts had a habit of leading Williams through mud and bogs or making her crawl under barbed wire, struggle through thick brambles, scramble down cliffs, or have to push aside herds of cows.

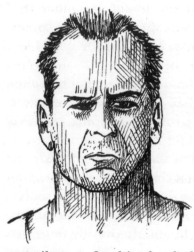

Willis, Bruce (American actor, b. 1955). In the long-ago days before every last celebrity on earth gave us the benefit of their insights on Twitter, Bruce Willis was a keen participant in the *Ain't It Cool News* online discussion forum. Posting as 'Walter B.' (his full name is Walter Bruce Willis), the *Die Hard* star was lambasted by other contributors for his slapdash approach to spelling and grammar. In response he wrote the immortal line, 'Proofreading is for pussies'.

Wilson, Harold (English politician and Prime Minister, 1916–95). In his own words: 'I see myself as a big fat spi-

194

der in the corner of the room. Sometimes I speak when I'm asleep. I might tell you to go to the Charing Cross Road and kick a blind man standing on the corner. That blind man may tell you something, lead you somewhere.'

Wing, Anna (English actress, 1914–2013). *See* O'Connor, Philip

Wishart, Alfred Wesley (American churchman and historian, d. 1933). Wishart's 1900 book, *A Short History Of Monks And Monasteries*, gave an intriguing glimpse of some of the goings-on in medieval monastic life: 'Two monks took the blood of a duck, which they renewed every week; this they put into a phial, one side of which consisted of a thin, transparent crystal; the other thick and opaque; the dark side was shown until the sinner's gold was exhausted, when, presto! change, the blood appeared by turning the other side of the phial. Innumerable toe-parings, bones, pieces of skin, three heads of St. Ursula, and other anatomical relics of departed saints, were said to cure every disease known to man.'

Wittgenstein, Ludwig (Austrian-British philosopher, 1889–1951). Wittgenstein was born into one of the richest families in Europe, but gave all his money away, and, in the final years of his life, chose to work as a hospital porter and laboratory assistant. His brother Paul was a concert pianist, who continued to perform after having his right arm amputated during the First World War. Composers including Ravel, Britten, Hindemith and Prokofiev all wrote pieces especially for him. *See* Popper, Karl

Woulfe, Peter (Irish chemist and alchemist, 1727–1803). Woulfe was described as 'the last alchemist'. His rooms in London were crammed with scientific apparatus including retorts, crucibles, and alembics, together with mysterious boxes, packages, and crates. He took his breakfast at four o'clock in the morning and occasionally invited friends to join him, though they had to use a secret signal to gain admittance. Whenever he fell ill, Woulfe's remedy was to travel in the mail-coach from London to Edinburgh and back again.

Wright, Orville and Wilbur (Pioneers of flight, 1871–1948 and 1867–1912). The first journalist to witness the Wright brothers' piloting their Flyer biplane published his story in *Gleanings In Bee Culture*, a magazine for beekeepers.

Zardari, Asif Ali (Pakistani politician, b. 1955). When serving as President of Pakistan between 2008 and 2013, Zardari had a black goat ritually slaughtered at his house in Islamabad every day. Denying newspaper reports that the goat sacrifice was designed to protect against black magic and the Evil Eye, his official spokesman explained that the practice gave pleasure to God, and in any case, goats were not killed every day, just 'quite often'.

Zatopek, Emil (Czech long distance runner, 1922–2000). Zatopek was one of the twentieth century's greatest long-distance runners, described by journalists variously as 'like a man who had been stabbed in the heart', 'as if his next step would be his last', and, definitively, 'like a man wrestling with an octopus on a conveyor belt'.

Zevon, Warren (American musician, 1947–2003). On his deathbed, Zevon asked his son to destroy his porn collection before his wife found it. Unable to resist viewing the material first, Zevon Junior was disconcerted to discover that it consisted entirely of home movies featuring the singer-songwriter playing the male lead.

Zugun, Eleonore (Rumanian spirit medium, 1913–?). Eleonore Zugun was known as 'the Spook of Talpa'. She had an invisible familiar named Dracu, who bit and scratched her but could be propitiated with gifts of chocolate cake. She became a popular phenomenon in London and Vienna, until her supernatural powers vanished when she hit puberty. Later, she became a hairdresser.

BIBLIOGRAPHY

Dictionary Of National Biography (DNB)
The Catholic Encyclopaedia 1907 (TCE)

Ackroyd, Peter, *The English Ghost* (Vintage, 2011).
Aldous, Richard, *The Lion And The Unicorn: Gladstone Vs Disraeli* (Pimlico, 2007).
Allen, David Elliston, *The Naturalist In Britain* (Penguin, 1978).
Altick, Richard D., *Victorian Studies In Scarlet* (Norton, 1970).
American Woman, *The Ladies' Vase or, Polite Manual For Young Ladies* (Parsons, 1849).
Amis, Martin, *Koba The Dread: Laughter And The Twenty Million* (Cape, 2002).
Arnold, Catharine, *Necropolis: London And Its Dead* (Simon & Schuster, 2006).
Arthur, T. S., *Grappling With The Monster, or, The Curse and the Cure of Strong Drink* (Lovell, 1877).
Attlee, James, *Nocturne* (University of Chicago, 2011).
Aubrey, John, *Miscellanies Upon Various Subjects* (John Russell Smith, 1857).
Babbage, Charles, *Passages From The Life Of A Philosopher* (Pickering, 1994).
Baily, F. E., *Six Great Victorian Novelists* (MacDonald, 1947).
Bair, Deirdre, *Samuel Beckett: A Biography* (Cape, 1978).

Baker, Phil, *Austin Osman Spare: The Life And Legend Of London's Lost Artist* (Strange Attractor, 2011).

Bangs, John Kendrick, *The Booming Of Acre Hill* (Harper, 1902).

Barbellion, W. N. P,. *The Journal Of A Disappointed Man* (Chatto & Windus, 1919).

Barber, Lynn, *Mostly Men* (Viking, 1991).

Baring-Gould, Sabine, *Curiosities Of Olden Times* (J. T. Hayes, 1869).

——, *The Vicar Of Morwenstow* (Methuen, 1939).

Barker, Hugh, *Hedge Britannia: A Curious History of a British Obsession* (Bloomsbury, 2012).

Beauclerk, Charles, *Nell Gwyn* (Macmillan, 2005).

Beeton, Isabella, *Mrs Beeton's Book Of Household Management* (Oxford, 2000).

Bell, Rudolph M. & Mazzoni, Cristina, *The Voices Of Gemma Galgani* (University of Chicago, 2003).

Bennett, Arnold, *Literary Taste: How To Form It* (Hodder & Stoughton, 1909).

Bird, J. Malcolm, *Margery The Medium* (Small, Maynard, 1925).

Bird, John, *Percy Grainger* (Elek, 1976).

Blacker, Terence, *You Cannot Live As I Have Lived And Not End Up Like This: The Thoroughly Disgraceful Life And Times Of Willie Donaldson* (Ebury, 2007).

Blakeston, Oswell, *Sun At Midnight* (Anthony Blond, 1958).

Bloy, Léon, *Le mendiant ingrat* (Société de Mercure de France, 1908).

Blunt, Wilfrid, *England's Michelangelo* (Hamish Hamilton, 1975).

Boswell, James, *The Life Of Samuel Johnson* (Oxford, 1953).

Brendon, Piers, *Eminent Edwardians* (Martin Secker & Warburg, 1979).

——, *Eminent Elizabethans* (Jonathan Cape, 2012).

Brooke, Christopher, *The Saxon And Norman Kings* (Batsford, 1963).

Bugliosi, Vincent, *Reclaiming History: The Assassination Of President John F. Kennedy* (Norton, 2007).

Burke, Carolyn, *Becoming Modern: The Life Of Mina Loy* (University of California, 1997).

Butler, Alban, *Lives Of The Saints, Vol. 5* (Burns & Oates, 1996).

Caine, Hall, *My Story* (Appleton, 1909).

Cameron, Agnes Deans, *The New North: Being Some Account Of A Woman's Journey Through Canada To The Arctic* (Appleton, 1910).

Casson, Herbert N., *The History Of The Telephone* (A. C. McClurg, 1922).

Chalmers, Thomas, *A Series Of Discourses On The Christian Revelation, Viewed In Connection With The Modern Astronomy* (John Smith, 1817).

Chang, Jung & Halliday, Jon, *Mao: The Unknown Story* (Cape, 2005).

Collins, Paul, *Banvard's Folly* (Picador, 2001).

Colquhoun, Ithell, *Sword Of Wisdom: MacGregor Mathers And 'The Golden Dawn'* (Neville Spearman, 1975).

Cornwell, John, *Hitler's Pope: The Secret History Of Pius XII* (Viking, 1999).

Costello, Peter, *Jules Verne: Inventor Of Science Fiction* (Hodder & Stoughton, 1978).

Cruse, A. J., *Matchbox Labels Of The World, With a History of Fire-Making Appliances from Primitive Man to the Modern Match, together with a History of the World's Labels* (Robert Ross, 1946).

Dallas, E. S., *Kettner's Book Of The Table* (Dulau, 1877).

Darwin, Charles, *The Life And Letters Of Charles Darwin* (John Murray, 1887).

Daston, Lorraine & Park, Katharine, *Wonders And The Order Of Nature 1150–1750* (Zone, 2001).

Davies, Dido, *William Gerhardie: A Biography* (Oxford, 1990).

Davies, Marion, *The Times We Had: Life With William Randolph Hearst* (Ballantine, 1975).

De Ligne, Charles, *Melanges militaire, litteraires et sentimentaires* (1807).

De Quincey, Thomas, *The Works Of Thomas De Quincey* (Pickering and Chatto, 2000–03).

Dingwall, E. J., *Some Human Oddities: Studies In The Queer, The Uncanny And The Fanatical* (Home & Van Thal, 1947).

——, *Very Peculiar People: Studies In The Queer, The Abnormal, and The Uncanny* (Home & Van Thal, 1950).

D'Israeli, Isaac, *Curiosities Of Literature* (Edward Moxon, 1843).

Diverse Hands, *The Lives, Opinions & Remarkable Sayings Of The Most Famous Ancient Philosophers, translated from the Greek of Diogenes Laertius* (1688).

Donne, William Bodham, *Old Roads And New Roads* (Chapman & Hall, 1852).

Doyle, Arthur Conan, *The Original Illustrated Strand Sherlock Holmes* (Wordsworth, 1989).

Dumas, Alexandre, *Dictionary Of Cuisine* (W. H. Allen, 1959).

Edmonds, David & Eidinow, John, *Wittgenstein's Poker* (Faber, 2005).

Edwards, Jill, *Personality Pointers* (Permabooks, 1950).

Elliot, R. H., *The Myth Of The Mystic East* (Blackwood, 1934).

Evans, Admiral Sir Edward, *British Polar Explorers* (Collins, 1946).

Fadiman, Anne, *Ex Libris: Confessions Of A Common Reader* (Penguin, 1999).

Falk, Bernard, *The Naked Lady, or Storm Over Adah: A Biography Of Adah Isaacs Menken* (Hutchinson, 1934).

Field, Eugene, *The Love Affairs Of A Bibliomaniac* (Cosimo, 2012).

Finch, Christopher & Rosenkrantz, Linda, *Gone Hollywood* (Doubleday, 1979).

Firbank, Ronald, *Inclinations* (Grant Richards, 1926).

Fleming, Fergus, *Barrow's Boys* (Granta, 1998).

Foster, William Trufant ed., *The Social Emergency: Studies In Sex Hygiene And Morals* (Houghton Mifflin, 1914).

Fulford, Roger, *Hanover To Windsor* (Batsford, 1960).

Fuller, O. E., *Brave Men And Women: Their Struggles, Failures, And Triumphs* (H. J. Smith, 1884).

Gardiner, A. G., *Certain People Of Importance* (Jonathan Cape, 1926).

Gardiner, John Eliot, *Music In The Castle Of Heaven: A Portrait Of Johann Sebastian Bach* (Allen Lane, 2013).

Gardner, Martin, *Fads & Fallacies In The Name Of Science* (Dover, 1957).

Gilbert, T. et al., *The Arabian Art Of Taming And Training Wild And Vicious Horses* (Henry Watkins, 1856).

Gill, William Fearing, *Edgar Allan Poe After Fifty Years* (Arena, 1899).

Goddard, Jimmy, *Cosmic Friends* (STAR Fellowship, undated).

Goldring, Douglas, *South Lodge: Reminiscences of Violet

Hunt, Ford Madox Ford and the English Review Circle (Constable, 1943).

Goodman, Jonathan, *The Killing Of Julia Wallace* (Scribner's, 1969).

Goodman, Matthew, *The Sun And The Moon: The Remarkable True Account Of Hoaxers, Showmen, Dueling Journalists, And Lunar Man-Bats In Nineteenth-Century New York* (Basic Books, 2010).

Gosse, Edmund, *Portraits And Sketches* (Heinemann, 1912).

Gottlieb, Sidney ed., *Hitchcock On Hitchcock: Selected Writings And Interviews* (University of California, 1997).

Gould, John M., *How To Camp Out* (Scribner, Armstrong, 1877).

Gould, Nat, *The Magic Of Sport* (John Long, 1909).

Gould, Stephen Jay & Purcell, Rosamund, *Finders Keepers: Eight Collectors* (Norton, 1992).

Grann, David, *The Lost City Of Z* (Doubleday, 2009).

Grant, John, *A Directory Of Discarded Ideas* (Corgi, 1983).

Grant Duff, Mountstuart E., *Notes From A Diary 1851–1872* (John Murray, 1897).

Gravil, Richard et al. ed., *Coleridge's Imagination* (Cambridge, 1985).

Greenberg, David, *Nixon's Shadow* (Norton, 2004).

Gross, John, *The Rise And Fall Of The Man Of Letters* (Macmillan, 1969).

Guides at the Dickinson Homestead: Nancy Harris Brose, Juliana McGovern Dupre, Wendy Tocher Kohler, and the Resident-Curator, Jean McClure Mudge, *Emily Dickinson: Profile Of The Poet As Cook, With Selected Recipes* (Dickinson Homestead, 1976).

Hall, Trevor H., *The Strange Case Of Edmund Gurney* (Duckworth, 1964).

Hanna, Abigail Stanley, *Withered Leaves From Memory's Garland* (1857).

Harvey, John, *The Plantagenets* (Batsford, 1948).

Hawkes, Jacquetta, *A Land* (Cresset, 1951).

Henricks, Gordon, *Eadweard Muybridge: The Father Of The Motion Picture* (Secker & Warburg, 1975).

Heppenstall, Rayner, *Reflections On The Newgate Calendar* (W. H. Allen, 1975).

——, *The Intellectual Part* (Barrie & Rockliff, 1963).

Hill, Christopher et al., *The World Of The Muggletonians* (Temple Smith, 1983).

Himmelfarb, Gertrude, *Victorian Minds* (Weidenfeld & Nicolson, 1968).

Hochschild, Adam, *King Leopold's Ghost* (Macmillan, 1999).

Hoffman, Paul, *Wings Of Madness: Alberto Santos-Dumont And The Invention Of Flight* (Hyperion, 2003).

Holliday, Robert Cortes, *Walking-Stick Papers* (Doran, 1918).

Holloway, Mark, *Norman Douglas: A Biography* (Secker & Warburg, 1976).

Hopkins, Gerard Manley, *Poems And Prose* (Penguin, 1953).

Hopkins, Matthew, *The Discovery Of Witches* (1647).

Horn, Henry J., *Strange Visitors, A Series Of Original Papers, Embracing Philosophy, Science, Government, Religion, Poetry, Art, Fiction, Satire, Humor, Narrative, And Prophecy, By The Spirits Of Irving, Willis, Thackeray, Bronte, Richter, Byron, Humboldt, Hawthorne, Wesley, Browning, And Others Now Dwelling In The Spirit World, Dictated Through A Clairvoyant, While In An Abnormal Or Trance State* (1871).

Horne, Alistair ed., *Telling Lives* (Macmillan, 2000).

Houdini, Harry, *Miracle Mongers And Their Methods: A Complete Exposé Of The Modus Operandi Of Fire Eaters, Heat Resisters, Poison Eaters, Venomous Reptile Defiers, Sword Swallowers, Human Ostriches, Strong Men, Etc* (Dutton, 1920).

Houellebecq, Michel, *H. P. Lovecraft: Against The World, Against Life* (Weidenfeld & Nicolson, 2006).

Hughes, Rupert, *The Love Affairs Of Great Musicians, Volume 1* (L. C. Page, 1903).

——, *The Love Affairs of Great Musicians, Volume II* (L. C. Page, 1904).

Illies, Florian, *1913: The Year Before The Storm* (Clerkenwell, 2013).

Ireland, Alleyne, *An Adventure With A Genius: Recollections Of Joseph Pulitzer* (Lovat Dickson, 1938).

Jameson, Anna Brownell, *The Diary Of An Ennuyée* (Saunders & Otley, 1838).

Jay, Ricky, *Learned Pigs & Fireproof Women* (Robert Hale, 1987).

Jennings, Hargrave, *Curious Things Of The Outside World: Last Fire* (T. & W. Boone, 1861).

Jones, Dan, *The Plantagenets* (Harper, 2013).

Jung, C. G., *Memories, Dreams, Reflections* (Flamingo, 1995).

Kennett, White, *A Register and Chronicle Ecclesiastical and Civil* (1728).

Kenyon, J. P., *The Stuarts* (Batsford, 1958).

Kokoschka, Oskar, *A Sea Ringed With Visions* (Thames & Hudson, 1962).

Kurth, Peter, *Isadora: The Sensational Life Of Isadora Duncan* (Little, Brown, 2001).

Lahr, John ed., *Joe Orton: The Complete Plays* (Methuen, 1976).

Lamont, Peter, *The First Psychic: The Peculiar Mystery Of A Notorious Victorian Wizard* (Little, Brown, 2005).

Lavay, Jerome B., *Disputed Handwriting: An Exhaustive, Valuable, And Comprehensive Work Upon One Of The Most Important Subjects Of To-day* (Harvard, 1909).

Leapman, Michael, *The World For A Shilling* (Faber, 2011).

Leverton, Mrs Waldemar, *Small Homes And How To Furnish Them* (Pearson, 1903).

Levin, Bernard, *Taking Sides* (Jonathan Cape, 1979).

Lewis, Roger, *Charles Hawtrey 1914–1988: The Man Who Was Private Widdle* (Faber, 2001).

Lloyd, Alan, *The Wickedest Age* (David & Charles, 1971).

Lombroso-Ferrero, Gina, *Criminal Man, According To The Classification Of Cesare Lombroso Briefly Summarised By His Daughter, Gina Lombroso-Ferrero* (Putnam's, 1911).

Lynd, Robert, *The Pleasures Of Ignorance* (Methuen, 1930).

MacGregor, John M., *Henry Darger: In the Realms of the Unreal* (Delano Greenridge, 2002).

Machen, Arthur, *The London Adventure or The Art Of Wandering* (Martin Secker, 1924).

Mackay, Charles, *Extraordinary Popular Delusions And The Madness Of Crowds* (Harrap, 1956).

Mailer, Norman, *Oswald's Tale* (Random House, 1995).

Manning, William, *Recollections Of Robert-Houdin, Clockmaker, Electrician, Conjuror* (Chas L Burlingame, 1898).

Martin, Iain, *Making It Happen: Fred Goodwin, RBS, And The Men Who Blew Up The British Economy* (Simon & Schuster, 2013).

Maxtone-Graham, John, *Safe Return Doubtful: The Heroic Age Of Polar Exploration* (Constable, 2000).

McKechnie, Samuel, *Popular Entertainments Through The Ages* (Sampson Low Marston, 1931).

Meiklejohn, J. M. D. & M. J. C., *A School History Of England And Great Britain* (Meiklejohn & Holden, 1920).

Mencken, H. L., *The Diary Of H. L. Mencken* (Knopf, 1989).

Mendel, Arthur P., *Michael Bakunin: Roots Of Apocalypse* (Prager, 1981).

Michell, John, *Eccentric Lives & Peculiar Notions* (Adventures Unlimited, 1999).

Miller, Stephen, *The Peculiar Life Of Sundays* (Harvard, 2008).

Monk, Ray, *Ludwig Wittgenstein: The Duty of Genius* (Free Press, 1990).

Moody, A. David, *Ezra Pound: Volume One* (Oxford, 2007).

Moore, Tim, *Do Not Pass Go: From The Old Kent Road To Mayfair* (Yellow Jersey, 2002).

Morris, Christopher, *The Tudors* (Batsford, 1955).

Mowbray, Jay Henry, *Sinking Of The Titanic* (Dover, 2003).

Nashe, Thomas, *Strange Newes, of the Intercepting Certaine Letters* (1593).

Newcomb, Harvey, *A Practical Directory For Young Christian Females* (Massachusetts Sabbath School Society, 1851).

Newsome, J. ed., *Pliny's Natural History: A Selection From Philomen Holland's Translation* (Clarendon, 1964).

Newton, Michael, *Savage Girls And Wild Boys: A History Of Feral Children* (Faber, 2002).

Nicholl, Charles, *A Cup Of News: The Life Of Thomas Nashe* (Routledge & Kegan Paul, 1984).

——, *Somebody Else: Arthur Rimbaud In Africa 1880–91* (Cape, 1997).

Nicolson, Adam, *Power and Glory: Jacobean England and the Making of the King James Bible* (HarperCollins, 2003).

Norton-Kyshe, James William, *The Law And Customs Relating To Gloves, Being An Exposition Historically Viewed*

Of Ancient Laws, Customs, And Uses In Respect Of Gloves, And Of The Symbolism Of The Hand And Glove In Judicial Proceedings (Stevens & Haynes, 1901).

O'Connor, Richard, *Ambrose Bierce: A Biography* (Victor Gollancz, 1968).

O'Donnell, Elliott, *Strange Cults And Secret Societies Of Modern London* (Phillip Allan, 1934).

Oxonian, An, *Thaumaturgia, or Elucidations Of The Marvellous* (Edward Churton, 1835).

Paxman, Jeremy, *The Political Animal* (Penguin, 2007).

Pearsall, Ronald, *The Table-Rappers* (Joseph, 1972).

Pearson, Hesketh, *Conan Doyle* (Methuen, 1943).

——, *Extraordinary People* (Harper & Row, 1965).

Penrose, Barrie & Courtiour, Roger, *The Pencourt File* (Secker & Warburg, 1978).

Pimbley, Arthur Francis, *Pimbley's Dictionary Of Heraldry* (Pimbley, 1908).

Pite, Ralph, *Thomas Hardy: The Guarded Life* (Picador, 2006).

Plomer, William ed., *Kilvert's Diary: Selections From The Diary Of The Rev. Francis Kilvert* (Cape, 1944).

Plumb, J. H., *The First Four Georges* (Batsford, 1956).

Price, Harry, *Stella C.: An Account of Some Original Experiments in Psychical Research* (Souvenir, 1975).

Purcell, William, *Onward Christian Soldier: A Life Of Sabine Baring-Gould* (Longmans Green, 1957).

Radford, Edwin ed., *Encyclopaedia Of Phrases And Origins* (Clare, 1950).

Rice, Edward, *Captain Sir Richard Francis Burton* (Scribner's, 1990).

Richardson, John, *Sacred Monsters, Sacred Masters* (Cape, 2001).

Robb, Graham, *Rimbaud* (Picador, 2000).

Rogers, Byron, *The Last Englishman: The Life Of J. L. Carr* (Aurum, 2003).

Rogers, Samuel, *Recollections Of The Table-Talk Of Samuel Rogers* (Edward Moxon, 1856).

Rose, Phyllis, *Parallel Lives: Five Victorian Marriages* (Alfred A. Knopf, 1983).

Ross, Alan, *Reflections In Blue Water: Journeys In The Gulf Of Naples And In The Aeolian Islands* (Harvill, 1999).

Ross, Peter, *The Curious Cookbook* (British Library, 2012).

Ruskin, John, *Fors Clavigera* (George Allen, 1871–84).

——, *Praeterita* (Everyman, 2005).

Schwartz, Peter ed., *The Ayn Rand Column* (Second Renaissance, 1991).

Shattuck, Roger, *The Banquet Years* (Cape, 1969).

Shaw, William, *Inside Britain's Cults: Spying In Guru Land* (Sage, 1995).

Sheldon, May French, *Sultan To Sultan: Adventures among the Masai and other tribes of East Africa* (Arena, 1892).

Shermer, Michael, *Why People Believe Weird Things* (Souvenir, 2007).

Silvester, Christopher ed., *The Penguin Book Of Interviews* (Penguin, 1994).

Singer, S. W. ed., *The Table Talk Of John Selden* (Reeves & Turner, 1890).

Sitwell, Edith, *Victoria Of England* (Faber & Faber, 1936).

Smith, Barry, *Peter Warlock: The Life Of Philip Heseltine* (Oxford, 1994).

Smith, Dodie, *Look Back With Love* (Heinemann, 1974).

Smythe, F. S., *British Mountaineers* (Collins, 1942).

Speedwell, Germander, *Sayings* (Unpublished manuscript, undated).

Staiti, Paul J., *Samuel F. B. Morse* (Cambridge, 1989).

Stirling, A. M. W., *Odd Lives: A Study of Conventions* (Macmillan, 1959).

Sutherland, John, *Lives Of The Novelists* (Profile, 2011).

Sweet, Matthew, *Inventing The Victorians* (Faber, 2001).

Symonds, John, *The Great Beast* (Mayflower, 1973).

Tabori, Paul, *Companions Of The Unseen* (Humphrey, 1968).

Taylor, Irene & Alan, *The Assassin's Cloak: An Anthology Of The World's Greatest Diarists* (Canongate, 2000).

Taylor, John, *Records Of My Life* (Edward Bull, 1832).

Theroux, Paul, *Sir Vidia's Shadow: A Friendship Across Five Continents* (Hamish Hamilton, 1998).

Tilbury, John, *Cornelius Cardew: A Life Unfinished* (Copula, 2008).

Timbs, John, *English Eccentrics And Eccentricities Volume II* (Richard Bentley, 1866).

——, *Things Not Generally Known* (Kent, 1860).

Topsell, Edward, *The History Of Four-footed Beasts And Serpents* (1607/08).

Trollope, Fanny, *Domestic Manners Of The Americans* (Whittaker Treacher, 1832).

Untermeyer, Louis, *Lives Of The Poets* (W. H. Allen, 1960).

Vignoli, Tito, *Myth And Science* (Kegan Paul, Trench, 1885).

Washington, Peter, *Madame Blavatsky's Baboon* (Secker & Warburg, 1993).

Waugh, Auberon, *Will This Do?: An Autobiography* (Arrow, 1992).

Wells, H. G., *Certain Personal Matters* (First World, 2007).

Wheen, Francis, *How Mumbo-Jumbo Conquered The World* (Fourth Estate, 2004).

——, *Tom Driberg: His Life And Indiscretions* (Chatto & Windus, 1990).

211

Wilkin, Karen ed., *Ascending Peculiarity: Edward Gorey On Edward Gorey* (Harcourt, 2001).

Williams, Margo, *Out Of The Mist: More Adventures Of An Isle Of Wight Psychic* (Self-published pamphlet, 1982).

Williams, W. E. ed., *A Book Of English Essays* (Penguin, 1951).

Wilson, Colin, *The Devil's Party: A History Of Charlatan Messiahs* (Virgin, 2000).

Wishart, Alfred Wesley, *A Short History Of Monks And Monasteries* (Albert Brandt, 1900).

Wooldridge, David, *Charles Ives: A Portrait* (Faber, 1975).

Wyndham, Horace, *Mr. Sludge, The Medium* (Bles, 1937).

——, *This Was The News: An Anthology Of Victorian Affairs* (Quality Press, 1948).

Zevon, Crystal ed., *I'll Sleep When I'm Dead: The Dirty Life And Times Of Warren Zevon* (Ecco, 2007).

Ziegler, Philip ed., *From Shore To Shore, The Final Years: The Diaries Of Earl Mountbatten Of Burma 1953–79* (Collins, 1989).

SOURCES

The formidable scholarly rigour of this book is fatally undermined, I am afraid, by the fact that there are several gaps in the list of sources given below. Some of my earlier gleanings first appeared on the Hooting Yard website, and I am afraid I was not always diligent in noting down precisely where I had come across them. This is absolutely reprehensible, as reprehensible as the cow that attacked Mr Gladstone, but I hope I will not, like the cow, be shot. Rest assured I have not made anything up.

Abercrombie Moody
Abramovich *Popbitch*, 10 October 2013
Adam Baring-Gould, 1869
Adams, J. shine.yahoo.com/pets/presidential-pet-stories.html
Adams, R. Barber
Aladdin De Quincey
Albert Leapman
Alexandros decktheholidays.blogspot.co.uk/2011/05/strange-facts-of-how-famous-and.html
Alice *The Spectator*, 6 January 2001
Allegro the *Daily Telegraph*, 20 February 1988
American Woman American Woman

Amundsen Maxtone-Graham
Anderson Lamont
Anning Hawkes
Archer Gould, 1909
Armstrong Illies
Arthy *The Spectator*, 21 November 1940
Arthur Arthur
Atherton Wyndham,1948
Atholl Oakeley the *Daily Telegraph*, 8 January 1987
Aubrey Aubrey
Attlee Aldous

Babbage Babbage
Bach Gardiner, 2013
Baden-Powell Brendon, 1979
Bains Tilbury
Baird *DNB*

Bakunin Mendel
Balcolm Hanna
Ballard Channel 4 News, broadcast 20 April 2009
Bangs Bangs
Barbellion Barbellion
Baring-Gould Purcell
Barnes Richardson
Barrymore Finch & Rosenkrantz
Bastiat www.econlib.org/library/Bastiat/basSoph3.html
Bateman Mackay
Baxter martinnewell.stevedix.de/757
Bayliss the *Guardian*, 5 August 2002
Bechstein Timbs,1860
Beckett Bair
Beddoes Untermeyer
Beeton Beeton
Bell Casson
Bellas the *Daily Telegraph*, 3 June 2008
Benn Barber
Bennett Bennett
Bentham Grant Duff
Berkeley Smythe
Bernhardt the *Guardian*, 18 January 2014
Bertolotto Jay
Betty Timbs, 1866
Beverland Dingwall, 1950
Bierce O'Connor
Birch Taylor, 1832
Bisset Jay
Blair Wheen, 2004
Blake Timbs, 1866
Blears www.imdb.com/name/nm2234136/
Blegvad *The Believer*, December 2009

Blot digital.lib.msu.edu/projects/cookbooks/html/authors/author_blot.html
Bloy Bloy
Blunkett *Hansard*, 7 December 2004; the *Guardian*, 8 June 2009
Bohman *The Wire*, March 2002
Boswell Heppenstall, 1975
Bottle Jay
Boyle Daston & Park
Bradlaugh Nicolson
Bradshaw *Hansard*, 10 February 2005
Brahms the *Guardian*, 12 April 2001
Branden Shermer
Bristow the *Guardian*, 5 May 2009
Brooke, C. the *Daily Telegraph*, 6 March 2011
Brooker www.procolharum.com
Brooks the *Guardian*, 21 January 2014
Brown the *Daily Telegraph*, 7 August 1989
Buchanan *Buchanan's Journal Of Man, Vol. 1 No. 4*, May 1887
Buckland Allen
Burroughs the *Guardian*, 4 August 1997
Burton Kennett
Butler the *Guardian*, 10 December 2006
Byatt the *Guardian*, 25 April 2009
Byron, G. Untermeyer
Byron, W. Untermeyer

Cage www.cracked.com
Callaghan Wheen, 1990

214

Cameron Cameron
Capote Richardson
Cardew Tilbury
Carr Rogers, 2003
Caruso *The Believer*, June 2004
Casanova De Ligne
Casement Hochschild
Cash beyondthepoint.co.uk/2013
  /06/05/vange-well-no-5-3/
Chadwick the *Daily Telegraph*,
  7 January 1988
Chalmers Chalmers
Chamberlain Paxman
Charles I Singer
Chekhov *The Spectator*, 31 May
  1974
Chesterton G. K. Chesterton, 'A
  Piece Of Chalk', in Williams,
  1951
Christ *Private Eye*, 8 July 2005
Clark Goodman, 2010
C. L. S. *The Times*, 16 August
  1871
Coleridge Rogers, 1856
Collins, H.: Smith, 1994
Collins, W. Caine
Colman Finch & Rosenkrantz
Colonel De Quincey
Conolly Timbs, 1860
Coolidge Gardiner, 1926
Cooper Wyndham, 1948
Cowell www.cracked.com
Cowley *DNB*
Cradock thedabbler.co.uk/
  2013/10/food-in-the-sixties-
  the-enigma-of-mr-and-mrs-
  fanny-cradock/
Crandon Bird, 1925
Cravan Burke
Creevey Fulford
Crowley Symonds

Crowsley the *Guardian*,
  4 September 2009
Cruse Cruse
Cuif-Rimbaud Robb
Cutler the *Guardian*, 7 March
  2006

Damian Britten Sinfonia press
  release, 18 November 2013
Darger MacGregor
D'Arrigo the *Guardian*, 1 April
  2006
Darwin Darwin
Davies, M. Davies, 1975
Davies, P. M. news.bbc.co.uk/
  1/hi/scotland/4361079.stm
Davis Evans
Day *DNB*
Day-Lewis *Business Today*,
  9 March 2008
De André en.wikipedia.org/
  wiki/Fabrizio_de_Andre
De Bury Harvey
De Chasseneuz Baring-Gould,
  1869
De Clifford the *Daily Telegraph*,
  16 December 1987
De Gaulle *The Spectator*, 20 June
  2007
Delacroix Taylor, 2000
Della *The Young Englishman*,
  29 April 1876
Dellschau www.uh.edu/
  engines/epi1308.htm
DeMille Finch & Rosenkrantz
De Quincey De Quincey
De Southchurch Jones
De Worde Dallas
Dickens Lavay
Dickinson Guides
Dingwall Price

Dobson Meiklejohn
Donaldson Blacker
Donisthorpe gap.entclub.org/
taxonomists/Donisthorpe/
index.html
Donnelly Grant
Dorfeuille Trollope
Douglas Holloway
Doyle Pearson, 1943
Ducrow Arnold
Dufour Houdini
Duncan Kurth
Durham Gardner

Eddy Grant
Edgerly *The New York Times*,
19 August 1890
Edwards Edwards
Egerton Timbs, 1866
Eliot, G. Baily
Eliot, J. Nicholl, 1984
Eliot, T. S. Richardson,
Elliot, R. Elliot
Elliot, J. Timbs, 1860
Elizabeth I Nicholl, 1984
Eno hootingyard.org/archives/
11608
Erlik www.sacred-texts.com/sha/
sis/sis07.htm
Eve Gardner

Fabre Grant
Faith the *Guardian*, 13 May 2003
Felix Michell
Fewkes *The Journal Of American
Folklore*, October–December
1890
Field Field
Firbank Firbank
Fletcher *Slate*, 10 April 2013
Foote Radford

Ford Goldring
Fossmo the *Guardian*, 31 July
2004
Foster Foster
Franklin Fadiman
Frederick Plumb
Freeman the *Guardian*,
29 November 2006
Freud, L. *The Spectator*,
12 October 2013
Freud, S. Jung
Freytag-Loringhoven Burke
Friend the *Guardian*, 14 October
2008
Fripp *David Bowie: Five Years*,
BBC documentary, broadcast
25 May 2013
Fuller Fuller

Galgani Bell & Mazzoni
Galton Michell
Gandhi the *Guardian*,
28 November 2002
Garfunkel www.artgarfunkel.
com/library/list1.html
Garner Gardner
Gaudier-Brzeska Moody
Geisel examiner.com/article/10-
things-you-didn-t-know-about-
dr-seuss
Geller LWT/Granada television
broadcast, 2002
George I Plumb
George III Fulford
George V Fulford
Gerhardie Davies, 1990
Gibson the *Guardian*,
27 February 2010
Gillray Timbs, 1866
Gladstone Sitwell
Goddard, D. Goddard

Goddard, J. Goddard
Goering Horne
Goldsmith *The Spectator*,
  25 January 1975
Goodwin Martin
Gorey Wilkin
Gosse Allen
Gould Gould, 1877
Grainger Bird, 1976
Green mickhartley.typepad.com
  /blog/2008/11/hellfire-and-
  damnation.html
Grimaldi Timbs, 1866
Griswold Gill
Guinefort the *Guardian*,
  14 December 2013

Handl the *Daily Telegraph*,
  30 November 1987
Hardy *BBC News*, 15 October
  2013
Harmsworth Brendon, 1979
Harvey Nashe
Hauser Newton
Hawker Baring-Gould, 1939
Hawtrey Lewis
Haydn Hughes, 1903
Heiney *The Times*, 16 April 2008
Heliogabalus Dumas
Hemmerde Goodman, 1969
Henman BBC TV broadcast,
  7 July 2013
Henry VII Morris
Hensley the *Daily Mail*, 17 April
  2012
Heppenstall Heppenstall, 1963
Hericks the *Guardian*, 12 April
  2011
Herkomer Sweet
Heubeck the *Guardian*,
  25 October 2009

Heurn Gould & Purcell
Hewson the *Mail On Sunday*,
  10 October 2009
Hibberd *DNB*
Hitchcock Gottlieb
Hitchens the *Daily Mail*,
  31 December 2010
Hohman www.sacred-texts.com/
  ame/pow/pow105.htm
Holliday Holliday
Holmes Doyle
Home Wyndham, 1937
Hope the *Guardian*, 25 March
  2004
Hopkins Hopkins, 1953
Horn Horn
Horniman www.lewcock.net/
  index.php?ption=com_content
  &task=view&id=78&Itemid=85
Howard the *Guardian*, 3 March
  2008
Howerd the *Daily Telegraph*,
  20 April 1992
Hubbard Gardner
Hübner *Harper's New Monthly
  Magazine*, Vol. 2, No. 12,
  May 1851
Hudson Evans
Hugh of Lincoln *TCE*
Hughes, H. en.wikipedia.org/
  wiki/Howard_Hughes
Hughes, T. Baker
Huston the *Guardian*, 18 January
  2014

Ilg Nicholl, 1997
Ives Wooldridge

Jacobs the *Guardian*, 22 January
  2014
James I Timbs, 1860

217

James II Kenyon
Jameson Jameson
Jansson Blakeston
Jantjie the *Guardian*,
  12 December 2013
Jennings Jennings
Jeronima Exhibition Guide, *The
  Sacred Made Real* (National
  Gallery, 2009)
Johnson Boswell
Jones Wilson
Jonsdottir the *Guardian*,
  23 December 2013
Joseph of Cupertino Dingwall,
  1947
Jung Heppenstall, 1963

Kafka *Slate*, 10 April 2013
Kaye martinnewell.stevedix.de/
  757
Keeler site.xavier.edu/polt/
  keeler/
Kennedy, J. *Vanity Fair*,
  November 2013
Kennedy, R. *The New York Times*,
  3 August 1962
Killick-Kendrick the *Guardian*,
  23 December 2011
Kilvert Plomer
Kim Jong-il mickhartley.typepad.
  com/blog/2011/10/may-
  prosper-the-era-of-the-workers-
  party.html
King Shaw
Kipling thedabbler.co.uk/2012/
  01/poetry-cake-exceedingly-
  plain-biscuits/
Kirchner *The Spectator*,
  18 January 2014
Knox *The Spectator*, 13 July 2013
Kokoschka Kokoschka

Laing Fleming
Lamarr *The Los Angeles Times*,
  28 November 2011
Lambert thedabbler.co.uk/
  2013/11/gef-the-talking-
  mongoose/
Landor Untermeyer
Laszlo Tabori
Lauri McKechnie
Lawrence *The Spectator*,
  9 September 1977
Leach Bugliosi
Leakey the *Daily Telegraph*,
  3 May 2013
Lear Ross, 1999
Lee the *Guardian*, 15 May 1997
Leigh-Pemberton the *Guardian*,
  26 November 2013
Lennon Levin
Leopold II Hochschild
Levasseur Allen
Leverton Leverton
Liberace the *Daily Telegraph*,
  5 February 1987
Lombroso Lombroso-Ferrero
Lotti Butler
Louis XV Timbs, 1860
Love the *Guardian*, 6 June
  2005
Lovecraft Houellebecq
Luckner Grann
Lutyens Washington
Lynd Lynd

Macbeth the *Guardian*,
  22 January 2014
Machen Machen
Malthus Himmelfarb
Mansfield Washington
Manning *The Spectator*,
  30 October 2004

219

Penn Hill

Persimmon the *Daily Telegraph*, 4 June 1896

Person www.thehistorymakers. com/biography/waverly-person-39

Pert www.bbc.co.uk/news/ magazine-13762313

Peter the Great Barker

Philby the *Guardian*, 8 July 2008

Philip news.bbc.co.uk/1/hi/ programmes/from_our_own_ correspondent/6734469.stm

Picasso *The Spectator*, 3 November 2007

Pierce www.logiston.com/ oddends/2008/11/ advertisement/

Pierrepoint the *Daily Telegraph*, 13 July 1992

Pimbley Pimbley

Pining hootingyard.org/archive/ sep04.htm#2004-09-02-2

Pitt Plumb

Pius XII Cornwell

Pliny Newsome

Poe Collins

Politianus Hughes, 1903

Pollock Wyndham, 1948

Pop *The Spectator*, 12 October 2013

Popper Edmonds & Eidinow

Pothorst hootingyard.org/ archive/sep04.htm#2004-09-02-2

Potter *The Times Literary Supplement*, 17 October 1980

Powell Gilbert

Powys thedabbler.co.uk/2014/ 01/the-madness-of-john-cowper-powys-or-strange-doings-at-phudd-bottom/

Presley the *Daily Telegraph*, 5 February 2013

Price Tabori

Pulitzer Ireland

Radcliffe Timbs, 1866

Raine BBC radio broadcast, 30 July 2008

Rajneesh the *Daily Telegraph*, 20 January 1990

Rand Schwartz

Rasputin www.jwz.org/blog/ 2013/05/rasputins-daughter-on-a-1935-wheaties-box

Ray BBC TV broadcast, 2006

Reichenbach *Harper's New Monthly Magazine*, Vol. 2, No. 12, May 1851

Richard II Harvey

Richet Pearsall

Robert-Houdin Manning

Robinson Finch & Rosenkrantz

Ross Mencken

Rossetti *The Spectator*, 2 June 1978

Rousseau Shattuck

Ruby Bugliosi

Rumwold canterburytalesfrom thefringe.blogspot.co.uk/2008 /07/we-arrive-at-st.html

Ruskin Ruskin, 2005

Russell the *Guardian*, 28 November 2011

Ruth The Truth the *Guardian*, 17 March 2006

Sadat Ziegler

Saintsbury Gross

Sand *The Spectator*, 5 March 2005

Satie Shattuck

Sayn-Wittgenstein Hughes, 1904

Scargill the *Guardian*, 1 March 2014

Schicklgruber Amis

Schieffelin *Scientific American*, 23 May 2008

Schleyer publicdomainreview. org/2012/10/17/truth-beauty-and-volapuk/

Scott, G. www.markpack.org.uk/ 13022/quite-simply-the-best-book-title-ever/

Scriabin Washington

Seward Pearson, 1965

Sheldon Sheldon

Shelley Untermeyer

Sherwood Goodman, 2010

Shiel Sutherland

Sibthorp Wyndham, 1948

Simpson the *Guardian*, 24 May 2012

Sivulla the *Guardian*, 6 August 2005

Smart mustardplaster.blogspot. co.uk/2010/11/bubble-squeak.html

Smith, A. Smythe

Smith, D. Smith, 1974

Smith, G. A. Hall

Smythe Smythe

Southey Gravil

Speedwell Speedwell

Speke Rice

Spencer, D. Brendon, 2012

Spencer, H. Harold Nicolson, 'Men's Clothes', in Williams, 1951

Spencer-Stanhope Stirling

Spinoza D'Israeli

Stanhope Stirling

Starr www.telegraph.co.uk/ gardening/chelseaflowershow /7763424/Chelsea-Flower-Show-2010-celebrities-at-Chelsea.html?image=1

Stein the *New Yorker*, 13 October 1934

Stephen Himmelfarb

Sterne *The Times*, 5 June 1969

Stevens www.kwls.org/littoral/ ernest_hemingway_knocked_ walla/

Stevenson *Edinburgh Evening News*, 11 November 2013

Stokes the *Daily Telegraph*, 12 May 1987

Struther *The Spectator*, 24 November 2001

Stuart *The Spectator*, 15 October 2011

Swedenborg Dingwall, 1950

Swinburne Gosse

Symmes Gardner

Taylor, E. the *Guardian*, 28 October 2009

Taylor, H. Rose

Tebbit the *Daily Mail*, 24 February 2010

Teed Gardner

Teilo Brooke

Thatcher *Maggie And Me*, Channel 4 broadcast, April 2013

Theophrastus Diverse Hands

Theseus Ruskin, 1871–84

Thornton Stirling

Tollemache-Tollemache the dabbler.co.uk/2013/10/the-rev-tollemache-tollemache-naming-names/

Topsell Topsell
Townson Timbs, 1860
Trollope Baily
Trotsky Moore
Tupper Collins
Tyson *City Journal*, 22 November 2013

Ure www.dickinsonranch.com/sale05.htm.

Van Dyke the *Guardian*, 11 November 2010; *Variety*, 19 August 2013
Van Vliet the *Guardian*, 19 December 2010
Vaughan longstreet.typepad.com/thesciencebookstore/2010/02/jf-ptak-science-books-llc-post-946——hell-broke-loose-or-the-notorious-design-of-the—wicked-ranters-discovered-on-sunday.html
Ventham *The Times*, 11 May 2013
VerEecke *The Plain Dealer*, July 1999
Verne Costello
Victoria Fulford
Vidocq V. S. Pritchett, 'The First Detective', in Williams, 1951
Vignoli Vignoli
Vinegar Tom Hopkins, 1647
Voliva Grant

Wallace Goodman, 1969
Walpole Lloyd
Warlock Smith, 1994

Warhol Richardson
Warner Ross, 2012
Waters Nicolson
Watts Blunt
Waugh Waugh
Wells Wells
Weschke the *Independent*, 23 February 2005
Wesley Ackroyd, *The English Ghost*
West Silvester
Whicker BBC TV broadcast, 1964
Whistler *The Spectator*, 22 February 2014
Wilde Wyndham, 1948
Wildman Timbs, 1866
Willcox *Now!* January 2006
William I Brooke
William IV Sitwell
Williams, K. the *Daily Telegraph*, 10 April 1988
Williams, M. Williams, 1982
Willis the *New York Observer*, 10 May 2007
Wilson Penrose & Courtiour
Wishart Wishart
Wittgenstein Monk
Woulfe Timbs, 1866
Wright Hoffman

Zardari the *Guardian*, 27 January 2010
Zatopek the *Guardian*, 23 November 2000
Zevon Zevon
Zugun Tabori